UNITY IS STRENGTH

TRADE UNIONS IN LATIN AMERICA
A CASE FOR SOLIDARITY

Latin America Bureau
Research and action on Latin America

**Researched and Written by
James Dunkerley
and
Chris Whitehouse**

First published in Great Britain in 1980 by

Latin America Bureau
P O Box 134
London NW1 4JY

A Bolivar Design

Map by Michael Green
Typeset by Bread 'n Roses, London NW1
Printed by The Russell Press Ltd., Nottingham

The cover illustration shows Bolivian miners armed
with dynamite in the popular mobilization that
overthrew the rightist military regime in October 1970.

Acknowledgements

We should like to thank the following people and organisations for their valuable help in the preparation of this book:

Alan Angell, Oscar Avila, Peter Chapman, Ian Cherrett, Chile Solidarity Campaign, Committee for Puerto Rican Independence, Contemporary Archive on Latin America, Colin Harding, John Humphrey, Alan Leather, Andrew Nickson, Raul Sohr.

We are particularly grateful to those Latin American trade unionists who have also helped us but who cannot be mentioned here by name for their personal safety. It is to them and their comrades that this book is dedicated.

A CALL FOR SOLIDARITY

The people of my country are struggling for their liberation against an economic system which exploits us and a bloody dictatorship which oppresses us. We know that international solidarity is necessary to guarantee not only our own final liberation but also the consolidation of the struggles and triumphs of other peoples in Latin America and the world. Concrete support through international solidarity is indispensable. If the blood of our heroes and martyrs nourishes the roots of victory, the active friendship of democratic peoples revitalises our hope. Through long years of struggle we have won the right to demand international solidarity. We wish to tell you that mere rhetoric is weak and ineffective in our struggle. We need material solidarity, we need to know who are our friends and who are our enemies; we want our enemies, who are the enemies of the people and of democracy, to be treated as your enemies also.

We recognise that the democratic peoples of the world have already shown international solidarity with the struggle of our people. But the time has come to broaden and deepen this support. United we are a force capable of winning the most enduring battle of our history. I commend this book to our British comrades as an important step towards understanding the nature of our struggle.

Miguel Angel Albizures

Member of the executive committees of the Confederacion Nacional de Trabajadores and the Consejo Nacional de Unidad Sindical, Guatemala.

London, April 1980

Miguel Angel Albizures (right) with Peter Tait, General Secretary of the Miners' International Federation.

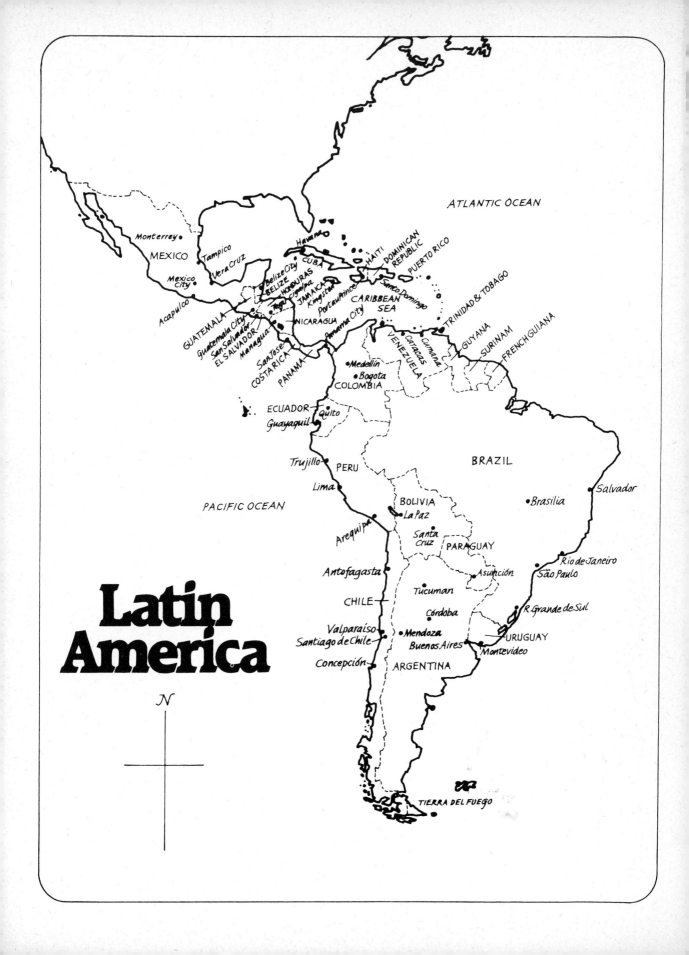

PART ONE

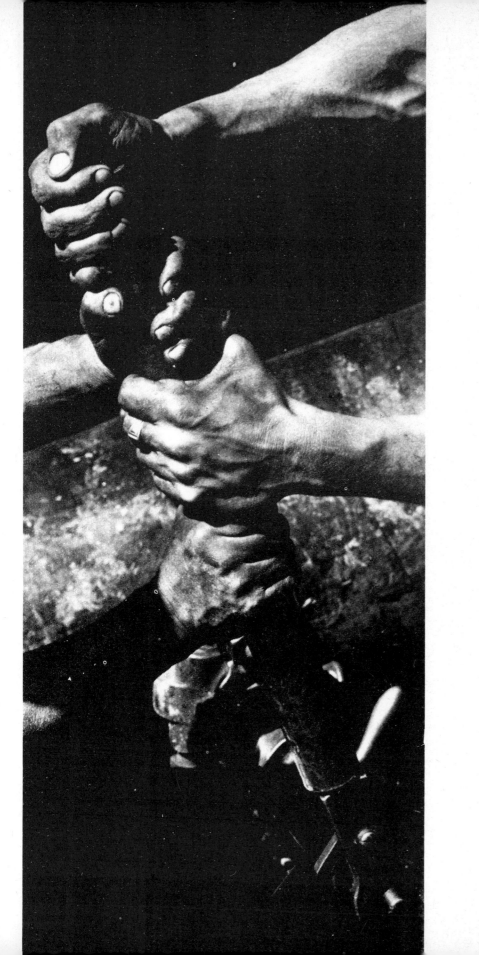

UNITY IS STRENGTH
INTRODUCTION

This book has been produced in response to requests from trade unionists and others engaged in solidarity work with Latin America who felt that there was no adequate general survey of trade unions in Latin America to help them campaign within the British labour movement. In the future we hope to produce more detailed studies on unions in specific sectors but here the main aim is to explain why British workers should be concerned about the condition of the Latin American labour movement as a whole.

Why Latin America?

Why Latin America? It is, after all, thousands of miles away; it does not appear to suffer from starvation as badly as do the Horn of Africa, Kampuchea or the Indian subcontinent; there are no major wars nor well-publicised boatloads of refugees; and there are no obvious ties with Britain.

From time to time natural disasters, such as major earthquakes in Guatemala and Nicaragua, or events such as the Chilean coup or the World Cup in Argentina attract the interest of the media. But in general Latin America receives little attention and European workers are left with a vague and distorted picture. Not surprisingly, this lack of awareness has meant that, with the exception of Chile, there has been little interest in or action on Latin America. However, there are very good reasons why British trade unionists should show solidarity with Latin American workers.

Poverty

There is no doubt that workers and peasants in Latin America live in extreme poverty. Unemployment is chronic, wages are low and rates of inflation high. As a result malnutrition, high mortality rates, disease and all the features of severe impoverishment are widespread. Chapter One shows that natural causes have very little to do with this state of affairs. It is the direct result of a global economic system in which wealth and power have become increasingly concentrated in the hands of multinational corporations in alliance with local capitalists at the expense of working people. The social cost of this system is most acute in underdeveloped or neo-colonial countries but it is by no means confined to them. Workers in North America, Europe and Britain are exploited by the system too.

British Links

Multinational corporations exist precisely because capital must grow and move to wherever it can make the highest profits: production and investment are shifted to the neo-colonial countries where labour is cheap and often kept so at the point of a gun.

Many such corporations operate in Britain and a substantial number are based here. There are at least a hundred British firms in Brazil, half that number in both Argentina and Chile and many more throughout the rest of Latin America. These include major companies such as EMI, ICI, Brooke Bond, Dunlop, Lucas, BP, Pilkington, Rank Hovis MacDougall, Bowaters, Plessey and Lloyds. The number of companies based in Japan, Europe and the USA that operate in both Britain and Latin America is very much higher. Ford, for instance, which we associate with Dagenham and Halewood, has plants in Venezuela, Uruguay, Mexico, Brazil and Argentina. In these cases British and Latin American workers are struggling against the same employer. Furthermore, British economic links with Latin America are growing, particularly in manufacturing industry, the sector which affects workers here most directly.

Repression and Chile

In September 1979 some 5,000 people turned out on the TUC demonstration in London in solidarity with the Chilean people on the sixth anniversary of General Pinochet's extreme right wing coup. They were demanding that the Conservative government, despite its obvious sympathies with the policies of the Pinochet regime, should not send an ambassador back to Santiago because of continuing repression in Chile. Many British trade unionists have been asked in branch meetings to aid fellow workers in Chile and in many cases this has gone beyond donations and messages of support. It has also included the 'adoption' of political prisoners, assistance for refugees, blacking and boycotting of goods and even the sending of union delegations to Chile to investigate conditions there.

The violent overthrow of President Allende's democratically elected socialist government in 1973 and the brutality of the repression that followed made such an impact on the European working class that it responded in a way not seen since the Spanish Civil War. No class conscious worker could fail to see the significance of the Chilean tragedy in which thousands died in order that the interests of big business be restored.

Every day basic human, democratic and trade union rights are violated throughout Latin America on a massive scale — workers' organisations and progressive forces are under constant attack. The Chilean coup was not an isolated event but part of a continuing offensive against the working class which began in earnest with the military takeover in Brazil in 1964 and continued with coups in Bolivia (1971), Uruguay (1973) and Argentina (1976). Military regimes also still prevail in

El Salvador, Guatemala, Honduras and Paraguay, and although the seven-year dictatorship in Bolivia was brought to an end with elections in 1978 the threat of another coup in that country remains strong.

A Tradition of Struggle

The present bitter struggle of the Latin American working class against dictatorship and exploitation is not new. Although the history of this struggle differs from that of the European or North American working class, the Latin American labour movement has a long tradition.

In Argentina, for example, the origins of trade unionism stretch back to the days of the British Chartists in the mid-19th century. By the turn of the century trade union organisations of some sort had been established in many countries and, as in Europe, the years following the Russian Revolution saw widespread militancy in Latin America and a spate of strikes in the more industrialised countries of the subcontinent. Thus, gains similar to those made by workers in Europe and North America were being fought for by workers in Latin America at the same time; most have still to be won. Part Two outlines the history of these struggles for each country.

International Organisation

The development of international trade union organisations has done little to remedy this state of affairs or provide the basis for authentic international union solidarity. In fact, in some cases these bodies actually serve the interests of the multinational corporations. The organisations are often in outright political conflict with one another and this has had particularly serious repercussions in Latin America.

The TUC plays an important role in the International Confederation of Free Trade Unions (ICFTU) and yet most workers in Britain are completely unaware of its existence, activities and record. Chapter Four looks at this important question which affects organised labour throughout the world.

Solidarity

Latin American workers are not just asking for sympathy but for class solidarity from their fellow workers in Britain and Europe. The low wages and oppression that Latin American workers suffer suit only the local entrepreneurs and multinational capital which readily takes jobs away from the highly unionised and much better paid workers of the industralised countries in order to make even greater profits. Workers in both Britain and Latin America are fighting exploitation and instances of collaboration in this joint struggle are becoming more frequent. Chapter Five considers the progress that has been made in developing union links and looks at the possibilities for further advance.

THE SYSTEM OF IMPOVERISHMENT

Latin America is rich in natural resources. It exports its minerals, foodstuffs and fuel to the 'advanced' nations, and some countries have undergone considerable industrial development. Nevertheless, Latin America remains undeniably 'underdeveloped' and most of its people continue to live an impoverished existence. At least half of the 330 million people that live in the sub-continent are considered by the UN to be destitute. Between 1960 and 1970 the poorest 40% of the population increased its annual income by only £10 per head. At the same time distribution of income has become increasingly one-sided — the rich have got richer and the poor have got poorer. For example, in Mexico the top 5% of income earners received 22 times as much as the bottom 10% in 1958 and 47 times as much in 1977.

Yet the US Department of Commerce reported that between 1950 and 1965 the flow of capital from Latin America to the United States was US $ 7.5 billions greater than the amount invested. British capital investment in this period was very much less but in 1974 it still made a return of 20%.

The domination of the Latin American economies by foreign capital is nothing new; high rates of profit were being made by British, French, German and US firms and banks well before the 19th century was out. In Mexico in 1910, 76% of the major companies were controlled by foreign investors. Investment, primarily by the US, but increasingly by Japan and Europe as well, has continued to grow and increased profits and control have followed.

Chuquicamata open cast copper mine in Chile. The Chilean economy is dependent on the export of copper. USPG

RETURN ON CAPITAL IN BRAZIL 1966-76

($ Millions)

Company	Inflow	Outflow
British American Tobacco	2.5	82.3
Johnson and Johnson	0.7	22.7
Esso	1.8	44.5
Firestone	4.1	50.2
Anderson Clayton	1.4	16.8
Rhone-Poulenc	14.3	60.6
Volkswagen	119.5	279.1
Pirelli	28.7	64.9
General Electric	13.9	19.4

U.S. PRIVATE INVESTMENT IN LATIN AMERICA ($ Billion)

1905	1.0
1925	3.9
1940	3.8
1946	7.2
1956	9.2
1965	14.3
1969	20.0

(NACLA, *The Yankee Dollar*)

Latin American economies have been shaped to the needs of the imperialist powers from the 16th century onwards. From the time of their political independence early in the 19th century Latin American countries became increasingly dependent on the export of raw materials and on the foreign capital that was concentrated in this key sector. This necessarily involved a close alliance between national and international capital but gave the former very little freedom of movement and left the Latin American economies highly vulnerable to fluctuations in world prices for raw materials.

This position has changed very little — the supply of cheap raw materials and basic foodstuffs remains critical to the industrialised countries. In periods of disruption of the world economy, such as the Depression and the Second World War, most Latin American countries began to manufacture consumer goods on a limited scale in order to reduce imports. This process became more widespread in the 1950s and was seen as a way of reducing their dependence. The post-war period, however, saw another even more important development: the rapid expansion of the multinational corporation which, attracted by low labour costs and the existence of large potential markets, gradually took over existing or set up new manufacturing industries, particularly in the relatively more advanced Latin American countries: Brazil, Argentina and Mexico. In Brazil, for example, labour costs in automobile manufacture account for only 10-15% of total costs; in Britain the figure is 30-35%.

This tendency of multinationals to expand abroad is particularly clear in the case of British companies. In 1979 foreign-based production accounted for 36% of the total output of the top fifty UK enterprises. Moreover, it increased more rapidly than domestic production and is now three

"So long, partner!"

DEPENDENCE ON KEY RAW MATERIALS 1959

Country	Commodity	% of total exports
Brazil	Coffee/Cacao	64
Chile	Copper	66
Colombia	Coffee	77
Venezuela	Oil	92
Bolivia	Tin	62
Argentina	Wheat/Meat	39
Uruguay	Wool/Meat	68

LATIN AMERICA'S SHARE OF U.S. IMPORTS OF KEY MINERALS 1969

Bauxite	99%	(Jamaica 58%; Surinam 23%; Dominican Republic 7%; Haiti 5%; Guyana 3%)
Manganese Ore	36%	(Brazil 35%; Guyana 1%)
Copper Ore	60%	(Chile 30%; Peru 30%)
Iron Ore	43%	(Venezuela 34%; Chile 4%; Brazil 3%; Peru 2%)
Lead Ore	31%	(Mexico 19%; Honduras 12%)
Zinc Ore	35%	(Mexico 25%; Peru 10%)
Petroleum (Crude)	31%	(Venezuela 27%; Bolivia, Chile, Colombia 4%)

(NACLA, *The Yankee Dollar*)

ELECTRICAL EQUIPMENT INDUSTRY. WAGES AND EMPLOYMENT IN SELECTED COUNTRIES, 1970

Country	Employment Total (000's)	Employment Production (000's)	Wages ($m)	Sales ($m)	Hourly Wages ($) (Production workers)	Wage Costs as proportion of sales
USA	1,840	1,237	14,756	48,137	3.82	.17
Britain	836	559	3,769	8,961	1.49	.21
W.Germany	1,095	774	6,028	13,888	2.59	.26
Brazil	107	84	151	1,014	.68	.091
Mexico	110	86	154	919	.42	.088

(US Senate Committee on Finance, *Implications of Multinational Firms for World Trade and Investment and for US Trade and Labor*, Feb 1973)

"I pledge allegiance to the flag of the country that gives me the best deal."

ation' means capitalisation which means production for profit and not need. Between 1964 and 1974, per capita production of food crops for domestic consumption fell by 10% while production of export crops (cotton, coffee, sugar, soybean, sorghum, etc.) grew by 27%. The result is less food and land for the rural population. Between 1950 and 1975 the number of landless peasants in Mexico rose from 1½ million to 5 million. In Brazil the increasing use of land for cultivation of soybeans for export meant a drastic reduction in land available to grow black beans, the staple food of the rural labour force, which as a result rose in price by 439% between 1974 and 1976. Every year half a million people flood into the city of Sao Paulo to escape poverty in the countryside.

Between 1960 and 1975, 33 leading US food processing companies made 335 new investments in the Third World, 80% times greater than their exports from the UK. The labour force of these firms in the UK has fallen by 6.4% in the last five years, whilst overseas employment has risen by some 5.5%. Between 1970 and 1976 British investment in Latin America rose from £2.1 million to £130.6 million — an increase from 10% to 20% of total UK investment in developing countries.

Within Latin America the process of industrialisation is very uneven, but in the most advanced countries it has become increasingly significant. In 1965, industrial products accounted for 8% of Brazil's exports; in 1979 this figure had risen to 35%. Brazil is now the world's tenth largest exporter of cars. In Mexico between 1950 and 1976 the industrial labour force grew from 12% to 18% and the agricultural labour force dropped from 58% to 33%. In Argentina two million people work in industry and only three quarters of a million in agriculture.

Multinational companies have also promoted the modernisation of agriculture in Latin America. On the face of it this would seem to be a positive step but, in practice, 'modernis-

SOME LEADING BRITISH COMPANIES WITH OPERATIONS IN LATIN AMERICA

AD International
Acrow Engineering
APV Holdings
Associated Portland Cement
Baker Perkins Holdings
Barclays Bank
Beecham Group
S and W Beresford
Booker McConnell
Babcock and Wilcox
Bowater Corporation
C T Bowring
British American Tobacco
Bridon
British Insulated Callenders Cables
British Northrop
British Oxygen
Brooke Bond Liebig
John Brown
Bunzl Pulp and Paper
Burmah Oil
Cable and Wireless
Coates Patons
Choride Group
Courtaulds
Croda International
Davy International
Decca
De La Rue
Delta Metal
Deltec International
Distillers
Dunlop
EMI
Expanded Metal
Foseco Minsep
General Electric
Gestetner
Grendon Trust
Guardian Royal Exchange
Guest Keen and Nettlefold
Guinness
Haden Carrier

Head Wrightson
Hill Samuel
Howard Machinery
ICI
J Johnson Management
Laporte Industries
Lead Industries Group
P Leiner and Sons
Letraset
Lloyds Bank
Lucas
Mather and Platt
McCorquodale
Mackenzie Hill Holdings
Marley
Midland Bank
Moling
James Neill Holdings
Ocean Wilson Holdings
Ofrex Group
Ozalid
Pearl Assurance
Permali
Phoenix Assurance
Plessey
Portals Holdings
Powell Duffrys
Pilkingtons
F Pratt Engineering
Reckitt and Coleman
Rio Tinto Zinc
Rolls Royce
Sears Holdings
Shell
Slater Walker
Spirax-Sarco Engineering
Spooner Industries
Standard Telephones and Cables
Stone Platt
Tate and Lyle
Tube Investments
Sun Alliance
Unilever
Union International
Wellcome Foundation
Wellman Engineering
Wilkinson Match

of them in Latin America. A reflection of this is that between 1965 and 1975, the use of fertilizer in the subcontinent trebled and the purchase of tractors increased by 75%. However, in Guatemala 87% of agricultural credit goes into the production of export crops and only 3% on the subsistence crops of rice, corn and beans; 81% of Guatemalan children suffer from malnutrition. Massey Ferguson entered Brazil in 1961 to produce tractors and was followed by Ford in 1974, but only the largest 2% of the country's five million farms possess both a tractor and a plough.

The effects of this mechanisation have been considerable. According to the ILO the current stock of tractors in Latin America displaces at least 2½ million workers. It is primarily US banks and corporations that control credit and the marketing of fertilizer, tractors, soya, coffee and bananas, but they are by no means alone; Tate and Lyle, British American Tobacco and Brooke Bond Liebig have played a major part in the impoverishment of the rural population of Latin America.

The cost to the workers of this multinational-promoted growth is extraordinarily high; if it were otherwise the multinationals would not find it profitable to invest. Increasing industrialisation and input of capital tell one story, the high rates of profit and poor working conditions tell another.

Agricultural workers on Costa Rica's cotton plantation. NACLA

BRITISH AMERICAN TOBACCO IN LATIN AMERICA

British American Tobacco is the third largest British-owned company (after British Petroleum and Shell if we consider world sales; and after British Leyland and General Electric if we look at employment). BAT employs over 200,000 people (only 40,000 in the UK) and its world sales were £4.3 billion in 1975. Over 91% of its profits come from outside the UK. BAT is the 11th largest non-US corporation in the world and the 27th largest if US transnationals are included.

Until 1960, BAT was a tobacco company alone. Now it has four divisions — tobacco, paper, cosmetics and retailing — of which tobacco is still the largest and most profitable.

Tobacco produces 65% of sales and 77% of the profits. BAT is the world's largest manufacturer of tobacco products, with factories in 50 countries and sales of its brands in 170 countries. BAT brands include Embassy, Benson & Hedges, Senior Service, Viceroy, Kool, Pall Mall, JPS, Gold Leaf, Lucky Strike, State Express 555, Players Medium Cut, etc. BAT owns 92 factories directly, and its affiliates have another 36.

Paper: Wiggins Teape is the core of the group's paper interests, which provided 8.6% of sales and 6.4% of profits in 1975. Paper subsidiaries exist throughout the world — 17 mills and factories in the UK, 5 in Belgium, France and Eire, others in Brazil and India, and 5 in Africa.

Cosmetics: Yardley, Lentheric, Morny, Cyclax, Scandia, Tuvache and Germaine Monteil are BAT's brands and constitute its cosmetics division. They account for only 1.7% of sales and 1.2% of profits; but are made in 38 countries and sold in 140.

Retailing: BAT is a major retailing organisation, selling £1 billion in 1975. 24% of sales and 9.5% of profits came from retailing. In England and Wales, BAT owns Homefare and International Stores and considers price controls to be responsible for its low profits; International threatened to close 350 of its 828 shops in June 1976. In the US, BAT owns Gimbels, Saks Fifth Avenue and 80% of Kohl (which has 88 stores). In Brazil, BAT owns 61% of Supermercados Peg-Pag which has 41 stores near Sao Paulo and Rio. In West Germany, BAT owns 26% of Horten, a chain of 57 stores.

BAT has a major presence in Latin America, particularly in Brazil. Latin America accounts for only 12.6% of world-wide BAT assets, but generates 22% of sales and 21% of profits. Of BAT's four divisions, tobacco accounts for 49% of assets, 65% of sales and 77% of profits.

BRAZIL

BAT owns 75% of Souza Cruz, which the *Financial Times* shows to be Brazil's second most profitable company. Souza Cruz has 80% of the Brazilian tobacco market and produced 80 million cigarettes in 1974. Its sales of £144 million gave Souza Cruz £39 million profits in 1974 —

a 27% rate of net profit. BAT's holding company, Cia Continental de Cigarros, which owns Souza Cruz, is the third largest foreign investor in Brazil (*Investors Chronicle* 4 July 1975). Over its 60 years in Brazil, BAT has invested only $2.5 million from outside Brazil and has re-invested Brazilian profits of $129.5 million, according to a recent investi-gation of multinationals in Brazil. BAT/Souza Cruz had the highest ratio of surplus to actual import of capital into Brazil of all the trans-nationals listed recently by the central bank for the period 1965-75. Profits reinvested *plus* profits re-mitted to British shareholders *plus* payments abroad for "technology" were $212 million, or 85 times as much as BAT put into Souza Cruz in all its 60 years. BAT remitted $81.3 million to its British shareholders in the last ten years.

Souza Cruz employs 16,000 people in Brazil, where the minimum wage is now 762 cruzeiros per month (roughly £40 per month) for 48-hour, six-day weeks. It has eight factories, and a ninth — nearing completion in Uberlandia, Minas Gerais — will be the largest in Latin America. Many small towns in tobacco growing areas are dominated by BAT/Souza Cruz processing mills. In 1975, for example, Souza Cruz bought some 100,000 tons of tobacco from 38,000 producers in Santa Catarina and Rio Grande do Sul for which they paid £25 million; just 12,000 tons, when exported, fetched £13 million. It is to be expected that BAT does not favour producer collectives or government selling arrangements!

Souza Cruz has a substantial min-ority interest in Aracruz Cellulosa, a company that is building a 400,000 ton per annum bleached pulp mill at Espirito Santo, 250 miles north of Rio. Wiggins Teape will take a corres-ponding share of its output.

In BAT's retail division, Super-mercados Peg-Pag have 41 stores around Rio and Sao Paulo. The 1975 BAT annual report speaks of un-satisfactory results due to price control and the decline of consumers' purchasing power.

In paper, BAT owns 100% of Cia Industrial de Papel Pirahy, which installed a sixth paper-making machine in 1975. In cosmetics, Yardley of London Brasiliera SAIC produced "encouraging" results.

CHILE
BAT's 1974 annual report recorded that its 50%-owned Cia Chilena de Tabacos SA "increased sales volume in a more stable situation: price increases led to a significant improve-ment in results in the latter half of the year". BAT had complained before the coup about "shortages of raw materials combined with con-trolled prices and uncontrolled wages".

ARGENTINA
BAT owns 85% of Cia Nobleza de Tabacos SAICyF (tobacco), and it wholly owns a paper company, SA Alejandro Bianchi y Cia Ltda, and a food company, SA Productora Avicola (SAPRA) ICAyG. In 1975, "despite the very difficult con-ditions" Nobleza improved its sales volume substantially and its market share. BAT also has 49% of Witcel SA FIA (paper).

COLOMBIA
Yardley of London Colombiana SA (69%).

MEXICO
Empresas La Moderna SA de CV (45%); Yardleys of London (Mexico) (100%).

VENEZUELA
CA Cigarrera Bigott Sucs (85%); Yardley of London Venezolana (100%).

COSTA RICA
Republic Tobacco Co (80%).

EL SALVADOR
Cigarreria Morazin SA (75%).

HONDURAS
Tabacalera Hondurena SA (80%).

NICARAGUA
Tabacalera Nicaraguense SA (60%).

PANAMA
Tabacalera Istmena SA (100%).

SURINAME
Tobacco Company of Suriname NV.

BARBADOS
British American Tobacco Co (Barbados) Ltd (100%).

GUYANA
Demerara Tobacco Ltd (70%).

JAMAICA
B & JB Machado Tobacco Co Ltd (69%).

TRINIDAD AND TOBAGO
The West Indian Tobacco Co Ltd (60%).

(CALA. 1977)

BROOKE BOND LIEBIG IN PARAGUAY

Brooke Bond Liebig is the main British company with subsidiaries in Paraguay, and through these subsid-iaries it has control over a large part of the country's economy. Brooke Bond Liebig and the US company Ogden Corporation together control almost all meat exports, which make up the chief exports of the country. Brooke Bond Liebig and Ogden Corporation together decide on the prices at which they buy cattle from farmers, and the very low level that they have fixed has contributed to a fall in the country's cattle popul-ation from 5.4 million in 1961 to 4.4 million in 1971. Brooke Bond Liebig slaughters 60,000 head of cattle a year.

Brooke Bond Liebig buys 60 per cent of the cattle it slaughters from independent farmers, and gets 40 per cent from its own ranches, which have a total area of 400,000 hectares.

Brooke Bond Liebig also own the air taxi company Taxi Aereo del Paraguay, and the meat packing plant at Zeballos-Cue. Each year 1,750 workers are employed in the meat packing plant for five months' seasonal work. Five hundred workers are employed on the ranches. None of these employees are covered by social security.

Strikes have been illegal in Para-guay since 1958. The trade unions are controlled by the right-wing Colorado party through the Confed-eracion Paraguaya de Trabajadores (CPT — Paraguayan Workers Confed-eration). This control is ensured by police violence at the election of union officials. Nevertheless the CPT put in a 30% wage claim for its mem-bers in Asuncion last October, a claim which was simply ignored. The Church backed Ligas Agrarias Crist-ianas (Christian Agrarian Leagues), the trade unions and the Liberal party have all been subject to a wave of repression unleashed in April 1976.

Brooke Bond Liebig is reportedly involved in speculative land purchases in areas due to be inundated when the Itaipu dam is complete. It is also reported that General Alfredo Stroessner, who came to power following the military coup of 5 May 1954, has been receiving payments from the company.

(CALA. 1977)

BRITISH INVESTMENT IN LATIN AMERICA

Net investment (flows) by United Kingdom companies in Latin America by country, 1970-1976 (excluding oil).

						£ millions	
	1970	1971	1972	1973	1974	1975	1976
Argentina	0.3	−2.1	7.8	2.6	6.1	8.7	18.5
Brazil	12.1	11.3	21.0	34.1	34.2	60.6	67.2
Chile	0.3	0.6	−1.6	−0.1	0.6	0.4	0.7
Colombia						1.4	2.5
Mexico	1.3	9.9	3.3	−5.8	3.1	6.6	2.1
Panama	0.1		1.3	0.8	3.4	−0.3	−2.1
Peru	0.3	0.5	−0.3			1.1	0.2
Uruguay	0.3			0.2	−0.2		0.2
Venezuela	0.1	−0.2	0.7	−0.1		1.8	0.6
Total	**10.4**	**20.0**	**32.2**	**31.7**	**47.2**	**80.3**	**89.9**
Latin America as % of developing countries	8.7	29.3	37.7	15.6	21.5	27.0	19.9

Net earnings of United Kingdom companies in Latin America, 1970-1976 (excluding oil).

						£ millions	
	1970	1971	1972	1973	1974	1975	1976
Argentina	4.9	2.5	6.2	8.3	7.6	9.4	22.1
Brazil	14.4	16.5	23.7	40.3	40.2	55.7	74.1
Chile	0.8	−0.2	−0.7	−0.3	0.9	0.8	−0.4
Colombia						1.1	2.9
Mexico	5.2	3.5	4.5	4.0	5.5	8.9	4.7
Panama	0.5	0.4	0.5	1.1	4.0	2.3	3.3
Peru	0.8	0.6	0.3	0.5	0.5	1.1	0.5
Uruguay	−0.1		0.1	0.2	0.2	0.2	0.3
Venezuela	0.5		0.9	0.6	0.3	2.2	1.9
Total	**27.0**	**23.3**	**35.5**	**54.7**	**59.2**	**81.7**	**109.4**
Latin America as % of developing countries	12.3	11.4	14.8	15.3	13.1	16.3	15.3

(*Overseas Transactions 1976*, Department of Industry, Business Statistics Office, HMSO, 1978.)

WAGES IN SELECTED COUNTRIES

1. ARGENTINA

Year	Real Wage
1960	100
1974	140
1975	145
1976	85
1977	75
1978	50
1979	35

(Derived from Labour Ministry data)

2. BRAZIL

i) Wages and Inflation 1968-76

Year	Increase in Min. Wage (%)	Cost of living Increase (%)
1968	22.9	43.0 (av)
1969	20.9	43.0 (av)
1970	19.9	43.0 (av)
1971	20.3	48.0
1972	19.1	47.0
1973	16.4	42.0
1974	20.5	104.0
1975	10.4	139.0
1976	28.2	171.0

(Fundacao Getulio Vargas)

ii) Hours of Work Necessary to Buy Basic Foods

Food	Quantity	Hours 1965	1971
Bread	6 kilos	7 hours 48 mins	13 hours 30 mins
Meat	6 kilos	26 hours 24 mins	42 hours 42 mins
Rice	6 kilos	3 hours 45 mins	6 hours 3 mins
Milk	7.5 kilos	4 hours 15 mins	5 hours 22 mins
Coffee	600 grams	46 mins	3 hours 23 mins

(DIESSE)

iii) Distribution of Income 1972

Income	% Population
Less than 1 min. wage	52.5
1-2	22.8
2-3	9.8
3-7	9.4
7-10	2.3
10 and over	3.2

(Sao Paulo: Growth and Poverty)

3. CHILE

Year	Real Wages
1972	100.0
1976	50.0
1977	57.5
1978	61.3

Wages and Inflation

In Latin America, as in much of the underdeveloped or neo-colonial world, the necessity of holding down labour costs and maintaining the freedom of capital has required the use of violence and the widespread establishment of military regimes. The result has been that while high levels of inflation have continued in Latin America the working class has been forced to suffer a large loss in earnings.

The assault on workers' living standards has been particularly acute in the countries ruled by military dictatorships. In Chile real wages have fallen by 40% since 1972; over 50% of the population depends on a family income of no more than £40 a month (the minimum wage) when, according to research by the unions, £112 is needed to provide the minimum requirements for the average family's healthy existence. Wages in Uruguay and Argentina have also plummeted and in Brazil workers have suffered a constant erosion of pay over the last decade. The official Brazilian system of linking the minimum wage to prices has not halted this as the figures have often been deliberately fixed or ignored by employers.

4. PERU

Year	Salaried Employees	Wage Earners	Govt. Employees	Min. Wage	Price Index
1973	100.0	100.0	100.0	100.0	100.0
1975	90.5	94.8	80.5	99.8	147.8
1977	65.1	72.2	59.0	79.5	283.2
1978	53.3	63.8	45.8	58.5	491.9
1979	48.6	68.5	38.5	80.7	774.3

(Resumen Semanal)

5. URUGUAY

Year	Real Wage
1971	100.0
1972	82.2
1973	81.5
1974	80.8
1975	73.6
1976	69.3
1977	61.1
1978	58.9
1979	56.0

(Banco Central)

INFLATION (%)

Country	1976	1977	1978	1979
Argentina	443.2	176.1	175.5	170.0
Brazil	41.9	43.7	38.7	77.2
Chile	211.9	92.0	40.1	38.9
Colombia	17.4	30.0	17.4	*25.0
Mexico	16.1	26.4	17.5	*20.0
Paraguay	4.5	9.3	10.8	*20.0
Peru	33.5	38.1	57.8	67.0
Uruguay	50.7	58.1	44.6	80.0
Venezuela	7.6	7.7	7.2	*20.0

(Inter-American Development Bank)
*Estimate

Even in countries without military regimes workers have suffered as a result of weak organisation, the strength of the large corporations, high unemployment, the antipathy of the state and the intervention of the police in disputes. In 1979, real wages in Mexico dropped for the third year running and in Colombia the 50% increase in the minimum urban wage was completely wiped out by price rises. The weekly earnings of a quarter of Colombia's working population are less than the price of a dozen eggs and a kilo of poultry. In 1974 the Guatemalan labour minister openly admitted that 80% of all wages would not satisfy even minimum nutritional requirements.

The odds are in your favour.

Newspaper advertisement of the Export Development Corporation, USA.

The Social Cost

This suppression of wages to near starvation levels has widened the already large disparities in wealth and has meant that the defence of the workers' economic position — the principal reason for the formation of trade unions — is no longer simply a central task but often a life and death mission.

The steep rise of food prices in recent years in Brazil has meant that those who exist on a minimum wage spend over 60% of their income on basic foods. In Peru the price of a loaf of bread rose 730% between 1973 and 1979 and workers' organisations have calculated that the average daily calorie intake has dropped over the last seven years from 2,200 to 1,752 (the internationally accepted basic level is 4,000). In Chile daily protein intake per capita has fallen from 53 units in 1970 to 43 units in 1979.

There is extensive malnutrition in Latin America and infant mortality rates are amongst the highest in the world; in several cases — most notably Brazil and Chile — they are actually rising. The situation is made worse by the widespread peddling of 'convenience foods' by the multinationals. Although notoriously unnutritious these are highly profitable, even in the Third World; 14 billion bottles of soft drinks are sold in Mexico every year.

URBAN MINIMUM WEEKLY WAGES IN SELECTED COUNTRIES 1979

Chile	£9.50
Costa Rica	£13.30
Dominican Rep.	£11.30
Ecuador	£12.70
El Salvador	£6.70
Venezuela	£13.30

(48 hour week. Ecuador and Venezuela now have an official 40 hour week. The above figures relate to 48 hours)

INFANT MORTALITY RATES

Country	%
Sweden	0.8
United Kingdom	1.4
Canada	1.7
USA	1.8
Cuba	2.2
Mexico	4.8
Costa Rica	5.9
Venezuela	6.3
Argentina	6.5
Chile	7.1
Guatemala	7.9
Brazil	8.2
Peru	11.0

(UNICEF)

Other statistics tell the same story. In Sao Paulo, one of the largest and fastest growing cities in the world, only 40% of the buildings have drains, only just over half have running water and less than 20% benefit from refuse collection. An Argentine paper recently claimed that over ten million litres of blood have been sold by the poorest and most marginalised sectors of the Latin American population — a macabre indicator of the level of exploitation to which they are subjected.

The miserable social security benefits provided by most Latin American countries, which in many cases are actually being cut back, have done nothing to alleviate this state of affairs. Most workers are excluded from retirement or redundancy benefits and where these schemes exist they often provide only a small fraction of the wage. In Chile, for instance, unemployment pay is £11 a month. In El Salvador only 2.7% of the population is included within the social security system; in Bolivia a large number of state employees still lack access to basic welfare facilities and in almost every country peasants are effectively excluded from any protection whatsoever.

In many countries expenditure on health and education has been cut to expand the military budget. In Brazil education took 5% of state spending and health 2% in 1974 while the military received 20%. In Chile the budgets for health and housing in 1978 were 68% and 82% lower than the figures for 1971; military spending rose 60% during the same period.

The World Health Organisation (WHO) stipulates that there should be one doctor for every thousand people for adequate health care to be available, but in Latin America only Uruguay and Argentina fulfil this requirement and even there medical facilities have been fast deteriorating. Also, the majority of doctors practice in urban areas, reflecting and further exacerbating the disparities in wealth and health

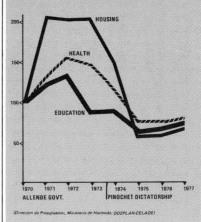

PUBLIC SPENDING ON HEALTH, HOUSING AND EDUCATION IN CHILE (1970 = 100)

HOUSING
HEALTH
EDUCATION

| 1970 | 1971 | 1972 | 1973 | 1974 | 1975 | 1976 | 1977 |

ALLENDE GOVT.   PINOCHET DICTATORSHIP

(Direccion de Presupuestos, Ministerio de Hacienda; ODEPLAN-CELADE)

The social cost of multinational-promoted growth. Millions of rural migrants are forced to live in shanty towns on the outskirts of Latin American cities, such as these squalid dwellings in Sao Paulo, Brazil. USPG

between town and countryside. As a result of the cutbacks in government spending in Peru enforced by the IMF, expenditure per patient in the workers' hospital is well below 50p a day; one social security official has described this hospital as 'hell's waiting room'. Doctors in La Paz, the capital of Bolivia where the infant mortality rate is 7.3%, say that hospital food contains less calories than the WHO minimum level for any person, sick or healthy. So poor is the Bolivian state, for example, that even when the country needs to treble the number of doctors to meet WHO minimum levels it cannot afford to pay all the doctors that already exist: in 1971 unemployment in the medical profession was over 25%.

POPULATION PER DOCTOR 1974

United States	750
United Kingdom	610
Uruguay	910
Peru	1,800
Bolivia	2,120
Colombia	2,180
Paraguay	2,340
Chile	2,420
Ecuador	2,840
Honduras	3,360
Haiti	8,510

(World Health Organisation)

A young boy carrying cotton on a Bolivian estate. Child labour is common throughout Latin America. CALA

Provision for education is no less appalling. In Guatemala there is one teacher for every 400 children of school age but one soldier for every 140 citizens. Out of a recent poll of nearly two million people over 25 years old, 93% had never attended school. In Ecuador, of each 1,000 children that enter primary school only 108 reach the first year of secondary education, 15 the first year of university and only one completes a university course.

Low school attendance does not simply reflect inadequate facilities; it is also because many families need to put their children to work as soon as possible in order to try and boost their income. According to a leader of the rank and file movement in Brazil, 'Obviously everybody in the family must work. Wives work. And kids can legally work at the age of

ADULT LITERACY 1974

Country	% Literate
Haiti	20
Bolivia	40
Guatemala	47
Nicaragua	57
Honduras	61
El Salvador	63
Ecuador	69
Peru	72
Colombia	74

(World Bank)

12. Employers like to employ them because they work hard and are classified as 'apprentices' and thus can be paid only half the minimum wage . . . 50% of the labour force is between 12 and 24 years of age.'

This does not mean that work is plentiful. Far from it. As elsewhere in the world, multinational corporations in Latin America cut costs by using capital-intensive technology which requires laying off workers and reducing the number of new jobs. Real levels of unemployment are masked by the high degree of underemployment (those who do not have a steady job). In Brazil and Mexico, the most industrialised countries in Latin America, unemployment and under-employment together account for 26% and 45% of the workforce respectively. In El Salvador the official unemployment figure is 35% but a rural worker can expect to work an average of only 141 days a year. In Chile, as a result of monetarist economic policies, jobs have been cut by the thousand. In the railway service alone 13,000 workers have lost their jobs in the last five years and the national rate of unemployment has risen from 8% in 1970 to 13.5% in 1978.

Historically the growth of manufacturing industry has not created greater employment in Latin America: in 1925 industrial production was 11% of total production; in 1967 it accounted for 23%; yet industrial employment remained at 14% over this entire period. In Peru, Chile and Colombia the number of industrial workers actually declined between 1950 and 1960. Between January and March 1977 nearly one-fifth of Ford's workforce in Brazil were fired and more have been laid off since. In Mexico production rose three times as much as employment in 1978. The government has announced a plan to create 2.2 million new jobs by 1982 but even if successful this will only maintain today's level of employment in percentage terms. It is estimated that by the end of the century less than half the economically active population of Mexico will have jobs paying the minimum wage or more.

In their search for ever greater profits corporations in Latin America have made increasing use of 'speed-up' (acceleration of production). Philips workers in Mexico claim that the rate of production was increased by 300% during 1973-74. Between 1971 and 1973 General Motors in Mexico increased output from 150 to 200 cars per day using the same equipment (a rise of 33%) yet over the same period wages were increased by only 15% and only 20% more workers were employed. In Brazil, 23% of the labour force suffer industrial accidents every year; in 1973, 59,000 workers were permanently injured and unable to work; 13,000 were killed. In Uruguay the figure for industrial accidents rose from 33,000 in 1968 to 42,000 in 1977; in 1978 there were over fifteen accidents for every hundred workers.

These, then, are the social costs of the system of impoverishment; its causes, however, are political as well as economic and the only possible response in such dire circumstances is a political one.

Unemployed rural workers in North East Brazil. USPG

Uruguay in 1973. Banner reads: 'Another lockout in TEM—500 families in the street'.

A SHORT LESSON ON EXPLOITATION

One of our leaders, a great man who was killed, once explained to us, in a very simple manner, the reason for our situation. He told us: 'Compañeros, the ten thousand workers of Siglo XX produce 300 or 400 tons of tin a month.' He took out a sheet of paper and continued: 'This represents what we produce, this whole sheet. This is all the profits we have produced in a month. How is this distributed?'

Then he tore the sheet into five equal parts. 'Of these five parts', he said, 'four go to the foreign capitalist. That's his profits. Bolivia only keeps one part.

'Now, this fifth part is also distributed according to the system in which we live, right? So, from this the government takes almost a half for transportation, customs and export expenses, which is another way to make the capitalist earn a profit, no? Because in our case, using our own trucks, wearing them out, we have to take our ore to Guaqui, on the border with Peru. In Peru there's a port. So, from there the ore has to go by boat to England, to the Williams Harvey foundry. From there it has to be transported by boat to the US, so that they can manufacture the things that later the other countries, even Bolivia, buy from the US at tremendously high prices. With all this, the capitalist once again gets almost half of this fifth of the profits that were ours.

'Then, of the half that remains, the government again grabs some, for its own benefit and for the following groups: the armed forces, for the salaries of the ministers, and to pay for their trips abroad. . . . Another part of it is used for repressive measures, for the army, the political police. . .

'And of the little bit that's left over, the government takes another part for social security services, for health, for hospitals, to pay for the electricity used by the people. Then another little part goes for the cheap groceries to keep the miners happy and contented. And they make us believe that we, by the 'goodness of the government', have price-frozen articles, bread, meat, rice, sugar . . . And so they take and they keep on taking. And, look, from all the money that tin brings in just a little bit remains, a little bit for the wages of the ten thousand workers who mined that tin.'

Domitila Barrios de Chungara
Let Me Speak

TRADE UNIONS IN LATIN AMERICA

AN OUTLINE BY ALAN ANGELL

The organisation and activities of trade unions in Latin America, the aims of their members and the intentions of their leaders may not seem so unfamiliar to someone with experience of European trade unions. But what is very different about labour movements in Latin America is the social, economic and political systems within which they operate. Unless this context is understood, it is pointless to try to put such questions as, for example, is the labour movement revolutionary or a relatively privileged group? Does it want widespread social change or simply disproportionate benefits for its members? Such seemingly straightforward questions are in fact not so simple even in the British context; they become much more complicated when asked about societies with huge disparities in income, status and power.

What is the working class in Latin American countries? Where does it end and the middle class begin? What is the relationship between a factory worker in a settled occupation, earning a reasonable income, and a street vendor, living in a shanty town and perhaps only recently arrived from the countryside? These questions are not merely statistical ones. They have great implications for our understanding of social class, and for political action.

Our immediate problem in trying to grasp the nature of the working class is the very small size of most industrial or manufacturing enterprises, and consequently the relatively small number of industrial workers employed in what is regarded as the 'modern sector'. In Chile close on half of all manufacturing workers are employed in firms of five workers or fewer; in Peru the average size of unions in manufacturing industry is only sixty one members; and even in Brazil in the 1960s firms of fewer than five employees represented about 70% of the total number of industrial firms. It is true that in some countries, such as Brazil, the manufacturing boom of the late sixties and seventies has increased very substantially the number of workers in large modern factories. But it is a mistake to think of small or artisanal enterprises as marginal, destined to disappear with economic progress. On the contrary, in many countries the number of artisanal firms is growing, often in a dependent relationship with large, often foreign-owned, capital-intensive plants. What is the class and political position of workers in these small enterprises? Their close relationship with the employer makes it easier for them to be controlled and obviously far more difficult for them to organise a trade union. But unless in some way or another they are associated with organised labour, either through industry wide federations, or politically through progressive parties, then the numerical strength and solidarity of the working class as a whole is seriously impaired.

Even more difficult to classify are workers who are self-employed, and who do not employ anyone else (apart perhaps from unpaid family labour). These people, neatly categorised as in the 'service' sector, lack stable employment and organisational structures, and often work immensely long hours for very little. Nor are their numbers insignificant. In Chile about 20% of the urban labour force is classed as self-employed; in Brazil nearer 30%. Yet their lack of involvement in trade unions does not mean that they cannot act with organised labour. On the contrary, as so much of union activity has to be political, rather than industrial, these self-employed workers can often (though not always) act as the allies of the unions in a common struggle against government austerity policies that affect the whole community, or against miserable living conditions that affect all the urban poor. But their association with organised labour tends to occur in times of crisis, born out of desperation, as in the general strike in Peru in 1977 against an increasingly repressive government, or in the famous *cordones industriales* (workers' defence committees) that developed in Chile in 1972 in order to defend the Allende government against attack from the bosses.

It is much more difficult to construct a continuing and permanent organisation involving all these sectors, especially as so many of the present authoritarian regimes in Latin America prohibit political activity.

A third related difficulty is the often tense relationship between the blue collar and white collar workers, between the wage earners and the salaried employees. A white collar worker enjoys a different

and better social security system to that of manual labourers; he operates under a different labour code and though he can often act in a militant way, he does not necessarily act radically. White collar workers are numerically important, rarely less than a third of the urban labour force, and many of them will be employed by the state. Very often they will seek political distance from the working class by associating themselves with a distinct political party. In Chile for example, while most manual workers were organised in the Socialist or Communist parties, the white collar workers were organised in the social democratic Radical party and later the Christian Democrat party, and of course they played an important role in the middle class opposition that did so much to bring down the Popular Unity government of President Allende.

In Peru for a long time they provided a strong element in the APRA party, a party that started on the left in the 1930s but one that has become much more right wing and opportunistic in recent decades. But one important group, the school teachers, who constitute the single largest (and perhaps most militant) union in Peru, are now largely dominated by Maoist leaders. Which way white collar workers will go politically is difficult to predict in advance; their militancy is often intense but their political commitment sometimes shows alarming inconsistency. This underlines once again the problem of constructing a solid and unified labour movement with a clear strategy and a commitment to class action.

There are two other points that must be made because they are crucial in affecting the labour market and in determining the political influence of the working class. Firstly, there is the very low rate of participation

Official unemployment figures disguise the high level of under-employment. This is a typical scene in Latin American cities; men and women of all ages eke out an existence by selling goods, such as cigarettes and matches, in the street.

BRANCH OF ECONOMIC ACTIVITY	AGRICULTURE, HUNTING, FORESTRY, FISHING	MINING, QUARRYING	MANUFACTURING	ELECTRICITY, GAS, WATER
UNITED KINGDOM 1977	2.5	1.3	28.5	1.3
WEST GERMANY 1978	6.2	1.3	34.6	0.8
ITALY 1978	14.2	← 24.9 →		0.9
ARGENTINA 1970	14.8	0.5	19.7	1.1
BOLIVIA 1976	46.2	4.0	9.7	0.1
BRAZIL 1976	36.2	← 16.5 →		
CHILE 1970	21.2	3.0	16.6	0.7
COLOMBIA 1973	25.9	0.6	11.4	0.4
COSTA RICA 1973	36.4	0.3	11.9	0.9
CUBA 1970	30.0	← 20.3 →		
DOMINICAN REPUBLIC 1970	44.3	0.1	8.1	0.1
ECUADOR 1974	46.5	0.4	11.5	0.5
EL SALVADOR 1978	41.0	0.3	14.2	0.5
GUATEMALA 1976	58.2	0.1	13.5	0.3
GUYANA 1965	29.6	2.8	15.1	1.3
HAITI 1971	61.5	—	5.1	—
HONDURAS 1977	60.9	0.3	12.0	0.3
JAMAICA 1978	29.1	0.7	10.5	3.6 (iv)
MEXICO 1979	40.1	1.5	18.2	0.4
NICARAGUA 1977	42.0	0.1	16.1	0.6
PANAMA 1970	38.4	0.1	8.0	0.9
PARAGUAY 1972	48.6	0.3	14.0	0.3
PERU 1972	40.9	1.4	12.5	0.2
PUERTO RICO 1979	5.7	0.2	19.2	1.4
TRINIDAD & TOBAGO 1978	12.2	← 18.4 →		←
VENEZUELA 1977	17.0	1.4	16.2	1.1

Notes (i) This includes 14.3% unemployed. (ii) includes storage and personal services. (iii) includes water.
(v) includes 4.5% working in the Canal Zone; in 1979 the US government handed over control of the Zone

CONSTRUCTION	WHOLESALE & RETAIL TRADE, RESTAURANTS & HOTELS	TRANSPORT, STORAGE & COMMUNICATION	FINANCING, INSURANCE REAL ESTATE & BUSINESS SERVICES	COMMUNITY SOCIAL & PERSONAL SERVICES	OTHERS
6.3	15.9	5.8	5.4	26.3	6.7
7.2	14.3	5.7	5.1	24.0	0.8
9.3	16.8	5.2	←——21.5——→		7.2
7.9	14.7	6.6	2.8	23.2	8.7
5.5	7.1	3.7	0.1	18.8	4.0
6.7	9.3	3.9	←——24.6——→		2.8
6.5	11.2	6.1	1.7	24.1	8.9
3.4	9.6	2.8	1.5	14.0	30.4 (i)
6.7	11.6	4.3	2.3	20.3	5.3
6.0	11.6 (ii)	6.1	←——24.6 (iii)——→		1.4
2.3	6.2	3.5	1.6	12.4	21.4
4.4	9.4	2.9	1.0	16.8	6.6
5.4	15.5	3.8	0.9	17.7	0.7
4.1	7.3	2.5	←——12.0——→		2.0
5.2	11.8	5.7	←——17.0——→		11.5
0.8	8.4	0.5	0.1	6.8	16.8
3.3	8.1	2.8	0.8	11.5	—
5.1	11.6	—	←——30.8——→		8.6
4.6	10.1	3.0	←——22.1——→		—
4.8	13.2	2.9	1.5	18.2	0.6
5.7	11.8	3.5	2.0	20.9	8.7 (v)
3.6	7.9	2.8	0.8	16.0	5.8
4.4	10.4	4.3	1.2	17.7	7.0
7.7	18.2	3.9	2.4	39.8	1.5
20.5 ——→ 16.2		7.3	←——23.6——→		1.8
8.8	17.4	6.7	4.1	26.2	1.1

iv) includes transport, storage and communication.
to the Panamanian government.

Statistics are not available for URUGUAY and BELIZE.
Source: ILO (*Year Book of Labour Statistics*, 1976, 1979).

of women in the wage-earning workforce.

Women generally make up less than 20% of the paid labour force; only in countries such as Panama and Colombia does the ratio of female to male workers approach that in western industrialised states. Moreover, the bulk of female employment is in domestic occupations, agriculture or the service sector, which accounts for two-thirds of the female labour force and is often no more than a euphemism for low-wage, non-unionised jobs such as street vending.

In general, wages for women are two to three times lower than those for men. In some countries there has been an appreciable increase in women in employment — in Brazil the percentage of women in the wage-earning labour force has risen from 13% in 1960 to 25% in 1979 — but, again, this increase has taken place in the most backward sectors. While only 16% of the total labour force in agriculture is female, in some regions, such as the Andes and north eastern Brazil, this figure is as high as 60%. Women, therefore, tend to be confined to domestic or rural labour and little involved in union matters. Their level of political participation is as a consequence usually lower or more conservative than that of men.

Secondly, trade unions are not confined to urban and mining areas; they also exist in the countryside along with a whole host of other organisations such as peasant leagues and movements, cooperatives, communal and ethnic associations. And in many Latin American countries the largest single occupational group are rural workers. There are, however, many different types of rural worker. Plantation workers, such as sugar workers in Peru or banana workers in Central America, are best seen as a rural proletariat working for a wage. These workers often form unions similar in nature and function to those of urban workers, whereas peasants mostly grow subsistence and sometimes cash crops on their own plots of land, tend to organise on the basis of locality and if politically mobilised are more likely to unite in a mass movement and engage in direct action rather than collective bargaining.

Generally speaking the contact between rural and urban labour is slight, even in countries which have had an advanced labour movement like Chile. Their aims are different, their work styles and communities often have little in common with urban labour. Sometimes they can be united through common association with a political party, but that is nowadays rarer given the widespread restrictions on party activity. A worker-peasant alliance may be theoretically necessary to make a successful revolution or even to construct a majority political

Indian women agricultural workers sowing seeds in Cochabamba, Bolivia. USPG

party, but, in practice, such an alliance still looks remote for most of the countries of Latin America.

Differences between Countries

The general point that will have emerged so far is the marked differences between the various groups that make up the working class of Latin America. But there are also great differences between the various countries. Argentina, for example, has as modern an occupational struct-

ure as many European countries, with a large proportion of its workforce in modern enterprises and only a small proportion working on the land. Argentine trade unions too, before government repression, were often comparatively wealthy, bureaucratic, industry-wide federations quite similar to those of Europe. Chile needs to be singled out, not because of the size or strength of its labour movement, but because of its radical political commitment, a commitment still strikingly alive in spite of

WOMEN IN STRUGGLE

The dispute in the Manufacturas Lolas plant in Lima, Peru lasted for well over a year and attracted much attention throughout the country. The owner, Jose Lolas, closed the plant on the pretext of a breakdown and tried to set up a 'yellow' union leadership which would accept many redundancies — 280 out of 380 workers, the vast majority of them women — and forego social security benefits for its members.

The same tactic had worked well in the Textiles Populares plant next-door which was also owned by Lolas. But the union in Lolas fought for legal recognition which it won together with a ruling by the ministry of labour that the factory must be reopened.

On 30 August when the workers returned they found that most of the machinery had been removed and it was impossible to restart production. A few days later workers in both

firms occupied the plants and held them for two weeks. On 19 September thugs hired by Lolas tried to force their way in and eject the women but they were held off and the occupations lasted for over six months. Despite the brutality of the boss's mercenaries and constant harassment by the police the workers maintained their position and eventually the management was forced to file a suit against them for 'usurping' the plant — they couldn't have been more cynical if they tried.

The women workers of Lolas have waged a fight not just against the management, the ministry of labour, hired thugs and the police but also against the backward and reactionary conceptions of their place in society. Violence against the woman worker very often comes from her own family, precisely where she should have firm allies. This is an invisible, forgotten, unpublished fight but it is just as hard and important.

Jornal, Lima, March 1979.

ASUNCION SOTOMAYOR, 42 YEARS OF AGE, SIX CHILDREN, GENERAL SECRETARY OF THE UNION:

'I had been put in charge of discipline in the union beforehand but I had so many problems I didn't want any job at all. My children always wanted me to be with them and they said that there were things that their grandmother or father couldn't deal with.

I had promised them that in future I would support the union but not take on any post. But the events leading up to the occupation and the occupation itself had an enormously important effect on me; I felt so furious at those who wanted to give in and side with the boss that at the meeting I accepted the job as general secretary.

I didn't say anything at home but with all the comings and goings and the constant meetings they realised something was happening and asked me. I told them that I just couldn't give up the fight like that. They cried and said, 'now you are the secretary you will be away from us even more.' I told them that a person has to fight not just for themselves but for others too. 'What would you do if they fired both your parents?' I said, 'wouldn't you fight back?' I had no choice because my husband was president of the union in Textiles Populares and they fired him. He backed me up, saying that every worker has to fight for the right to work and take on the boss in the only way he understands.

Some men, though, say to their wives 'It's either the factory or your husband and children. Leave the house and never come back.' Many women have given up the fight because it's on two fronts.'

strenuous government attempts to repress it since 1973. That radical commitment is the product of a long period of development of the left in which party and union activities were intertwined.

Although it is difficult to generalise, it is possible to make the following points.

Only in Argentina are the majority of urban workers organised in independent, sector-wide unions with a bureaucracy used to national collective bargaining. At present the union movement is under attack, but the movement is too powerful and representative to be repressed in quite the same way that it was, for a time at least, in Brazil, Uruguay or Chile.

Most other countries do have a number of powerful industry-wide federations but they organise only a small, sometimes privileged sector of the work-force, and can be rather detached from the general politics of labour (though that does not mean lagging behind; they can in fact be in advance). Petroleum workers, or miners, are by the nature of their occupations often isolated from the main urban centres. In Bolivia the tin miners have played a leading role in the politics of that country; but their militancy has hardly been typical of Bolivian labour, and neither has the miners' attachment to the politics of Trotskyism been spread outside the mines.

In Mexico and Brazil, economic development has recently seen the emergence of large and powerful unions — above all in the motor vehicle industry — but in these countries, until very recently, the structure of trade unionism was imposed by the government, and controlled by it, rather than an expression of workers' interests.

Generally in Latin America trade unions are small, weak, poor and hamstrung with all sorts of legal and political regul-ations imposed by governments, and intended to inhibit the development of a free and independent labour movement. The bargaining agent is the small local plant union, more often than not engaged in the long process of trying to stop real wages falling even more behind the usually high rates of inflation. Most workers, how-ever, are employed in firms too small even to have a union, and so are not covered by the minimal guarantees that an active plant union can bring. Labour relations inside many factories or in many firms are often paternalistic and the union, should one exist, is more

Back-breaking task of cutting cane.

or less company controlled. Job turnover in many Latin American countries is often very low, much lower than in Europe, and reflects the fact that reasonably paid, secure employment is a benefit not to be lightly discarded.

A general exception to this description are the state employees. The state in Latin America is often a very important source of employment and though in most countries there are provisions against state workers forming unions, in practice this is often ignored. State employees also have the advantage of being organised in large numbers, and facing one employer — the government, which has the power in theory to alter wage rates. State employees have emerged as some of the most militant groups in Latin America. School-teachers in a number of countries have followed a very combative policy against the government. But it is too simple to see in this militancy a political radicalism that could lend itself to the cause of overall worker unity. The intention of such militancy, at least in part, is to increase privileges compared with the urban manual work-force.

THE PRICE OF SUGAR

As investment in 'agribusiness' grows so too does the size of the wage-earning rural working class. Largely recruited from the peasantry, these workers suffer from particularly harsh exploitation and working conditions which in many cases are little better than those that prevailed when slave labour was used in the plantations.

Most of the work is seasonal — at harvest time — and involves the migration of large numbers of people, for example from El Salvador to Honduras or from Haiti to the Dominican Republic. The conditions in the Dominican Republic are so poor that even with an unemployment rate of 25% local workers resist taking jobs in the sugar plantations. The Haitian government, however, signs an agreement with the Dominicans for the employment of a certain number of its citizens at harvest time at wages of $1 per day.

These workers are under the control of military patrols who are supposed to deliver them back at the end of the season but instead they are very often 'sold' to the sugar companies with each soldier receiving a fee. A local army commander recently admitted that this took place but explained that soldiers were not to be blamed because they 'were acting on orders'. In eastern Bolivia many sugar workers are subject to a system of 'debt peonage' whereby they pay off loans made to them by the companies through their labour. Very often workers have no clear idea what the loan entailed and yet for the advance of a few dollars they may have to work for several years in order to clear themselves of an obligation from which they have no other escape.

In Guatemala the movement of labour on the big plantations is largely internal. Every year some 3-400,000 people are taken by contractors from the highlands to the fertile coastal plains to be housed in delapidated dormitories without sanitary facilities or electricity. Over 65% of the families who work on sugar plantations have an income that is inadequate to meet minimum nutritional needs.

The state of rural labour in Brazil is no better. In 1969 five million people were employed in coffee production and the number of agricultural day labourers has since grown. They work from ten to twelve hours a day, but are often away from home for 18, to earn between 50 cents and $1 per day. Because they are engaged on a daily basis, often far from home, and have to rely upon transport provided by contractors, union organisation is very difficult indeed. Nevertheless over 100,000 cane-cutters in Pernambuco, in the north-east, came out to win a 52% wage rise in October 1979. This was well below the 100% demanded but the strike was the biggest in fifteen years — an indication of the growing militancy of this extremely poorly paid sector.

Where plantation workers have developed some form of organisation and militancy to gain better conditions they are often subject to open repression. When workers in the Aztra sugar plant in Ecuador struck in October 1977 for a wage increase in line with the 20% rise in the price of sugar over 800 police were immediately sent in and attacked a mass meeting leaving 120 workers dead and over 200 wounded.

A month-long strike by 20,000 United Fruit workers in Costa Rica at the beginning of 1980 was only brought to a halt by the use of battalions of police who again shot on meetings and wounded scores of workers. Workers in five state-owned sugar plants in the Dominican Republic went on strike in January 1980 demanding enforcement of the minimum wage laws and the payment of bonuses of 30 days' pay to which they were legally entitled. The government offered only 15 days' pay in loans, immediately sent the army in to the major plants, banned all marches and sacked nearly 1,300 workers on the spot in open violation of the law and its own agreements.

In Central American countries such as Costa Rica, Panama, and Honduras, where the production of sugar, coffee, and citrus fruits is central to the economy, workers have increasingly become unionised and more combative but this process is still slow. Many more rural workers have no union at all or one that is controlled by the company or local government agents and useless from the point of view of defending their interests.

Unions, Politics and the State

It has been a persistent intention of governments in Latin America to curb the interests of the working class. Hence most countries have complex and elaborate labour codes, often enacted before organised labour was in any sense a political threat. As labour has become a political threat so the state has intensified its attempts to control or destroy labour movements.

Labour law regulates almost every aspect of union activity from collective bargaining to the way of selecting leaders. And if there is legal conflict, Latin American courts have shown themselves more likely to favour the government than the workers. But apart from control over the activities of labour, some governments have even determined the structure of union organisation. The Brazilian labour code for example, with the ministry of labour at the apex, lays down a very precise system of confederations, federations and local unions. And virtually all labour codes sanctify the difference between white and blue collar labour.

Apart from such open attempts to regulate labour, governments do not hesitate to employ other methods. The most notorious is that of repression; and instances are too sadly frequent of labour leaders being murdered in the interests of 'national security'. However, it may be questioned whether this is as effective a method of control as co-opting labour leaders by a system of patronage and corruption. For many years Mexican labour was led by men bought off by the government and notorious for their corruption (though this did not mean that they were inactive, especially if confronting an employer unpopular for some reason or another with the government). Labour can cooperate with progressive governments as it did with President Cardenas in Mexico in the 1930s. But the reality is that progressive governments are increasingly rare in Latin America, and what starts out as cooperation often ends as manipulation. The costs of surrendering political independence are high.

The intention of such detailed regulation of unions was to remove labour from politics; yet the consequences have been exactly the opposite. Because governments regulate so closely matters crucial to trade unions (income policies are an obvious example), unions must confront or try to influence governments if they are to achieve any of their basic objectives. Because legal regulation has made unions weak, they are forced to seek political allies to attempt to influence government policy. So in most countries in Latin America, trade unions are associated with one or another political party: Socialist, Communist or Christian Democrat in Chile; Peruvian sugar workers with the APRA, Peruvian schoolteachers with the Maoist left; Venezuelan peasant unions with *Accion Democratica*; the Mexican labour movement with the *Partido Revolucionario Institucional*, and so on. The major exception, once more, is Argentina, where a political movement, Peronism, was identified with the trade unions.

This close association with political parties brings advantages and disadvantages. The connection with a party can help to unify disparate occupational groups, it can bring together diffuse interests into a coherent strategy, it can aid and defend labour in crisis,

EXTRACTS FROM THE REPORT OF THE N.U.M. DELEGATION TO BOLIVIA 1979

The average basic wage is 36 bolivianos (about 80p). . . . Under the contract system people work up to 14 hours a day. . . . Officially miners work six eight-hour days a week to comply with the legal 48-hour week. Those who have worked 48 hours qualify to have Sunday off with pay. However, if a miner works Sunday, he is paid three times his basic wage and many miners find they have to do this in order to make ends meet. Indeed, most miners work three Sundays out of four.

When it is remembered that the miners often have families of seven or eight, it is no surprise that around 40% are 'topados' i.e. at the end of the month find they have no money to take home once their accounts for food at the company store have been paid. . . .

Miners returned to work far too soon after blasting — before the dust had settled — spurred, it seems, by the contract system of payment on rock tonnages moved. This unnecessary additional exposure to silicosis-provoking dust particles is compounded by exposure to the nitrous fumes from the blasting which are potentially more hazardous since they can cause emphysema which destroys the lungs.

There are usually four or five accidents a month. The less serious accidents include falling down a chute or a 'chimney' with a drill. . . . Since 1956 there have been 25,000 COMIBOL [the state mining corporation] employees afflicted with silicosis. In the block carving system, a miner tends to contract first grade silicosis within three to five years, second grade after five to seven years and third grade from seven to ten years (after which, if he is still alive, he is retired).

There are 2,600 workers in Siglo XX and 2,000 in Catavi employed by COMIBOL but only 1,000 houses in each town are provided. The company houses were built during the time of Patino (before the 1952 nationalisation of the mines). They have one room measuring 4m x 4m, a small patio of 2m x 2m and a small kitchen of 1½m x 1½m. There are usually at least eight people living in the house which has no toilet, no running water, and electricity for only limited periods. The rooms have no windows.

and it can act as a source of funds and of legal advice. But there are disadvantages too. Because more than one party competes for the support of labour, there can be sectarianism and the subordination of the interests of the unions to those of the party (and the best known example of this is probably that of APRA in Peru).

When a weak union movement needs an impetus towards unity, political differences can be a further dividing factor. And when political parties are suppressed and persecuted by repressive governments, then labour movements associated with such movements suffer as well. But it is obvious that the North American model of

apolitical unionism is totally misplaced in Latin America. Whether the US likes it or not, even the most basic expression of union activitiy is likely to be defined by Latin American governments as 'political'; and any attempt at collective action on behalf of the welfare of the poor is likely to be seen as subversive too.

For Guatemalan workers, Coca Cola's slogan 'The Spark of Life' has become 'The Spark of Death'.

THE FIGHT FOR A UNION: COCA-COLA IN GUATEMALA

Coca-Cola began its relationship with Embotelladora Guatemalteca (EG) in 1939 when it extended a licensing agreement to the Guatemalan firm. Since 1956, the company has been under the direct operating supervision of John C. Trotter, a lawyer, based in Houston, Texas. Although Coca-Cola does not appear as a direct owner of Embotelladora Guatemalteca, it still maintains control over operations through its licensing agreement with a responsibility towards workers at the plant.

Attempts to form a union were made in 1954 and 1968 but both times violently suppressed, the 'culprits' sacked and one leading militant kidnapped and executed.

1975

In August of 1975, conflict began when workers formed an ad hoc committee to organise a union for the purpose of gaining wage increases, and improving working conditions. At that time, the average worker earned between $2.08-2.50 per day (the legal minimum wage being $2.08 per day). This initiated the creation of a legally registered union toward the end of 1975 with the support of a majority of workers. During this few months' interim, the company attempted to prevent the formation of the union, threatening workers with loss of their jobs and offering money to union leaders to stop their organising activities.

In December, the company began to hire new workers from another region at $3.00 per day. They were

hired to act as a shock force to break the union from within. Many of these workers opted to join the union when they were told of the situation.

1976

In February, the company presented a dubious agreement, stating that workers did not want a union, first to the General Inspector of Labour who approved it, and then to the courts. It was signed by a number of workers from among those newly hired. Workers stated that they were coerced to sign this agreement upon threat of losing their jobs.

On March 25, the court announced a decision in favour of the company's agreement. Workers then proceeded to stage a sit-down strike on company property outside the plant. The company called in the police and in the process of forcibly removing the workers, 13 were seriously injured after being beaten and 14 were jailed. The company then fired 152 of the workers (all union members) who had participated in this action.

In early April, John Trotter met with union representatives declaring that he would never allow a union in his factory. A series of meetings then took place between the government, company, and union leaders. Subsequently, on April 7, the company agreed to accept back the 152 workers who had been fired.

On May 10, an accord was reached between the company and the union to consider a collective agreement. Negotiations dragged on for months with little progress.

During this time, the company, in its attempts to weaken the union organisation, set up 12 separate companies within the same plant, declaring it would not accept the executive committee of the union to represent workers in all 12 companies, but that collective agreements must be contracted with each separately.

The workers refused to continue negotiations until agreement was reached on a collective pact applicable to all of the separate companies.

In late 1976, several EG workers, actively involved in the union, were jailed for 165 days for the alleged killing of a policeman outside the plant.

1977

In March of 1977, two union members, Angel Villeda Moscoso and Oscar Humberto Sarti, escaped a murder attempt while driving in their car. These union members blamed the company, stating that they had received threats from the head of the industrial relations department of the Coca-Cola plant the previous December, to stop their union organising activities.

This was followed by another attempt at murder; this time against two labour lawyers, Luis Alberto Lopez Sanchez and Guillermo Monzon Paz, both of whom were seriously wounded.

In June of 1977, a prominent labour lawyer, Mario Lopez Larrave, was assassinated. He had been active in trying to extend the use of existing trade union laws. Soon after, another lawyer, Jorge Alfonso Lobo Dubon,

was also murdered. Both had worked closely with union leaders at the EG plant.

Despite these violent tactics, workers continued their struggle and late in 1977 it appeared that the Embotelladora Guatemalteca dispute was finally settled with the company granting recognition of a collective pact and an increase in wages.

1978

Then, beginning in December of 1978, a new onslaught of violence broke out when the company, in collaboration with the government, attempted to destroy the union's leadership.

On December 12, Pedro Quevedo, secretary for the union at EG, was assassinated. Following this, 23 workers were imprisoned on false charges while others have been threatened with death unless they sign petitions against the union.

1979

On January 30, 1979, Israel Marquez, general secretary of the CNT (National Confederation of Workers) and a leader of the EG union, requested political asylum within the Venezuelan embassy after repeated threats on his life, and at the beginning of March went into exile in Costa Rica.

On 5 April, Marquez's successor, Manuel Francisco Lopez Balan, was murdered while on his distribution round for the company in Guatemala City.

On April 20, Yolanda Urizar Martinez de Aguilar and Rosa Maria Wantlan Garcia, two leading trade union lawyers and advisors to the CNT, were arrested together with a CNT secretary. They were held for several days in Granja Penal de Pavon prison and then released. At the beginning of April, Yolanda Urizar had narrowly escaped a kidnap attempt.

1980

As a result of the campaign by the International Union of Food and Allied Workers, a visit by Israel Marquez to the Coca-Cola share-holders' meeting in the US, and the international outcry over the conditions in the Guatemala plant, Coca-Cola announced early in 1980 that Trotter's concession would be terminated.

An additional factor is the role and activities of international bodies. By this one means mostly North American influences whether directly, through mutual involvement in the regional trade union organisation ORIT, or indirectly through American-based training institutes such as the AIFLD, or clandestinely through the CIA. A great deal of money is spent by these groups in Latin America; rather less, though still a great deal, is spent by various Christian Democrat groups channelled mostly through another regional organisation, CLAT. However, one should not underestimate the capacity of some local labour movements to manipulate their much wealthier counterparts. But such activities are usually an intrusion into local politics and tend to reinforce the most reactionary and least class-based unions. Latin American unions want and need international solidarity, but they do not want to be forced to accept an ideological package, even if it is well financed.

Popular protest, involving but not exclusively confined to trade unions, came to dominate the politics of many Latin American countries in the 1960s and 1970s. To attempt to contain that protest — in Chile, Uruguay, Argentina, Bolivia and most recently in Peru — the state resorted to more drastic measures of repression and control under the guidance of authoritarian military regimes. Indeed, so strongly was the threat felt in some countries, that a deliberate attempt has been made to restructure the economy in such a way that the working class is less likely to pose a challenge in the future. The monetarist policies pursued in Chile by reducing the size of the manufacturing sector obviously weaken industrial unions.

Yet the greatest obstacle to the consolidation of these authoritarian governments still remains the labour movement. After ten years of industrial peace, 1978 saw massive and impressive strikes in Brazil. The Argentine military still faces the dilemma that has haunted governments in that country since the Second World War: how can the Peronist trade unions be incorporated into the political system in a way that neutralises their political strength and aims? A successful general strike in Peru hastened the military's decision to return the government to civilian hands. Even the bitter and savage repression of Pinochet's Chile has not destroyed the great political tradition of the union movement (the church too has played an important role in defending the basic rights of trade unions in Chile).

The policies pursued by many governments in Latin America are clearly detrimental to the interests of the vast majority of the people. As the most organised sector of the majority of the urban and rural poor, trade unions have been forced to speak for and to defend those interests. Trade unions have gone beyond their specific functions because the dominant system has made it extremely difficult to perform those functions with any degree of effectiveness. Unions must therefore offer an alternative social and economic model that overcomes differences inside the working class in order to confront a common enemy. The road is long and hard and there will be many reversals, but in a number of countries the first and perhaps most difficult steps have been taken. The first period of development of unions in Latin America in the early years of this century is known as the 'heroic stage'. The present period calls for efforts equally heroic.

(Alan Angell is University Lecturer in Latin American Politics and a Fellow of St. Antony's College, Oxford)

Argentine Generals Menendez and Bussi.

Where blood flows there is redemption. God is redeeming the nation through the armed forces . . . who have purified themselves in a Jordan of blood to stand at the head of the country.
Monsignor Victorio Bonamin,
Pro-Vicar of the Army.

. . . In Argentina, because of the state of siege, there may be people in jail who do not need to be tried. ADEPA [the journalists' union] should not feel itself under attack if there are one or two journalists in jail — there are also soldiers, doctors, lawyers, businessmen, industrialists and workers in jail for security reasons; we are all equal before the law.
General Harguindeguy,
Minister of the Interior, March 1977

While Videla governs, I kill.
General Luciano B. Menendez,
C.O. 3rd Army, Cordoba

ARGENTINA: THE VOICE OF REPRESSION

'. . . since then [the coup of March 1976] Dr Martinez de Hoz and his highly capable team have wrought marvels . . . now I leave Argentina firmly convinced that this rich and varied country has an especially bright future ahead of it . . . and shall do all I can to spread this message in London on my return.'
Mr Shakespeare,
former British Charge d'Affaires in Buenos Aires and now in charge of the Foreign Office's Caribbean and Central American Department

We shall promote the harmonious relationship between capital and labour through the strengthening of the employers' associations and the trade unions.
General Videla
30.3.76

The workers should know that the sacrifice demanded by the task of national reorganisation will be shared by all social groups.
General Videla
30.3.77

Argentine women protest, demanding to know what the military have done with their disappeared relatives.

THE STRUGGLE TODAY

Chile, workers demonstration in October 1972 against the first bosses strike. 'Against the Bosses' Stoppage—Workers to the Offensive!'

For over a century the Latin American ruling class in alliance with international capital attempted to increase the rate of exploitation and check the organisation of workers by manipulating the political system, which they controlled. Civil, democratic and trade union rights permitted, in theory at least, by the traditional liberal constitutions inherited from Europe and North America in the 19th century were either ignored or openly violated.

In the 20th century working class mobilisation was often defused by the granting of limited reforms such as basic social welfare and legislation on working conditions by populist regimes which actually increased the degree of state control.

However, the scale and depth of the economic crisis in the 1960s and 1970s, and the radicalisation of the peasantry and working class following the Cuban Revolution of 1959, meant that in many countries it was no longer enough simply to manipulate. The basic interests of the ruling class were at stake. The system as a whole had to be changed.

Military regimes took power by force in much of Latin America. Through the repression of the working class and progressive democratic sectors of society the interests of national and international capital were once again made secure. Long-established democratic rights were wiped out and today constitutions are being rewritten to put the final judicial seal on the new economic and political system.

The Chilean or Uruguayan generals may well refer continually to the 'will of the nation' or the 'mandate of the people' but everyone is fully aware that they have come to power through violence and destroyed political systems that, despite their considerable bias, were defended by organised labour because they offered at least some protection and the means to move forward.

The series of defeats suffered by the Latin American working class in the last decade and the wave of dictatorship that followed provide the most brutal proof that trade union activity has to be political if it is to have any profound and lasting effect.

The most immediate result of the dictatorships is the loss of rights to assembly, free speech and organisation. Workers in Argentina, Paraguay or Chile cannot meet and organise without the threat of a military raid, the kidnapping and 'disappearance' of leading activists, armed attacks on demonstrations and the ever-present fear of arrest and torture.

When miners in Yorkshire or South Wales take industrial action they may well suffer harrassment on the picket line. When miners in Bolivia strike they are beseiged by the army which cuts off the supply of food, water and electricity to the camp; in the past the workers and their families have been bombed and machine-gunned. When Peugeot workers in France come out they expect to suffer the hardship of loss of wages; when those who work for the same company in Argentina stopped work they were met by squads of soldiers before they even got out of the plant.

Paraguay has lived under a state of siege since the late 1940s; Guatamala has been ruled by right wing officers almost constantly since 1954. In Brazil the present dictatorship has held sway for over fifteen years and although the number of deaths run into hundreds rather than thousands, widespread arrests and torture have proved just as efficient as the massacres in Chile and the political killings and 'disappearances' in Argentina. The physical assault has been both longstanding— 20,000 dead in Guatemala from 1966-76 — and intensive — 20,000 killed in El Salvador in the first three months of 1980.

These are the most extreme examples; in other countries the level of violence has been lower and taken different forms but scarcely anywhere are active trade unionists free from the fear of physical attack. Because attention is rightly focussed on the most barbaric regimes it is often forgotten that every year there are political killings in countries such as Colombia, Ecuador, Peru or Honduras, and that in Guyana, 'The mere suspicion of one's being a member of an opposition party.. leaves one open to all kinds of harrassment, ranging from loss of one's job, unconscionable transfers in government employment, to the now famous death threat and violence'. (*Caribbean Contact*). Even in Costa Rica, which has something of a progressive image in Latin American terms, striking workers have been shot at. A 26-day strike by banana workers in January 1980 led to 150 arrests and many wounded when the Civil Guard opened fire on a meeting. The minister of labour supported the armed forces. 'We will do the same if other strikers try to stir up trouble,' he proclaimed.

The Labour Codes

In the last two years the major military dictatorships in Latin America have attempted to use the legal system in order to consolidate their anti-worker regimes through the revision of the traditional

'. . . the ever-present fear of arrest and torture'. A worker in the hands of the Chilean army.

POLITICAL REGIMES IN LATIN AMERICA

COUNTRY	REGIME	POLITICAL PRISONERS	DEATHS/ DISAPPEARED	INDEPENDENT TRADE UNIONS	COMMENTS
ARGENTINA	Military Dictatorship 1976	2,500-3,000 (1979)	8,000 deaths 15,000 disappeared (1976-79)	Repressed	Unions intervened; political activity banned; press controlled; anti-worker labour code.
BELIZE	British Colony Civilian/Parliament 1979			Legal	
BRAZIL	Military Dictatorship 1964	Less than ten. Amnesty 1979. Once 1,400	c.300 disappeared Number of deaths under torture unknown	Repressed	Extensive yellow union network. Anti-worker labour code based on Mussolini's fascist laws.
BOLIVIA	Unelected Executive/ Elected Parliament 1979*		c.250 in coup attempt Nov. 1979	Under Attack	Military dictatorship 1971-78: c.1,000 deaths; 1,000+ prisoners
CHILE	Military Dictatorship 1973	8,000 after coup. 1,000 arrests 1979	c.30,000 killed 1973. 2,500 disappeared	Repressed	c.300,000 political refugees. Anti-worker labour code
COLOMBIA	Military-backed Civilian 1978	c.1,000 (4,000 total in 1979)	c.100 Arrest & torture routine	Under Attack	Security Statute (1978) effectively suppresses democratic rights
COSTA RICA	Civilian/Parliament 1978		Rare	Legal	
CUBA	Communist Party Bureaucracy 1959	600 (several thousand released in 1979 amnesty)	Very few after insurrectionary phase.	Bureaucratically Suppressed	
DOMINICAN REPUBLIC	Civilian 1978	Some	Occasional	Under Attack	Invasion by US Marines in 1965 followed by US-backed Balaguer dictatorship until 1978 elections.
ECUADOR	Civilian/Parliament 1979	Amnesty 1979, but some remain.		Legal	Military dictatorship 1972-79; selective repression of unions.
EL SALVADOR	Military Dictatorship 1979	Unknown. Many arrests 1979	c.2,000 killed Jan-March 1980.	Repressed	Military in power since 1931

Country	Government / Year	Political Prisoners	Deaths	Trade Unions	Notes
GUATEMALA	Military Dictatorship 1978	Unknown	9,000 dead/disappeared 1978-79	Repressed	20,000 dead 1966-76 Military in control since CIA-backed invasion in 1954
GUYANA	Civilian Dictatorship 1966	Several	Unknown	Under Attack	Selective murder of opposition leaders by terror squads
HAITI	Civilian Dictatorship 1971	Unknown	Unknown, but estimated to be several hundred	Repressed	Duvalier family in power since 1957
HONDURAS	Military Dictatorship 1978	Unknown	Occasionally	Under Attack	Military regimes since 1972. Parliamentary elections April 1980.
JAMAICA	Civilian/Parliament 1976			Legal	
MEXICO	Civilian 1977	350-400	400	Legal	One-party state since 1934. Independent organisations face bureaucratic and sometimes violent attack.
NICARAGUA	Sandinista Junta 1979	7,500 — majority are members of National Guard of former regime	c.40,000 during civil war 1978-79	Trade union federation organised by Sandinista junta; opposition discouraged.	
PANAMA	Military-backed Civilian 1968	Very few	Occasional	Legal	
PARAGUAY	Military Dictatorship 1954	Several hundred released in 1978 amnesty, but arrests continue.	Several hundreds	Repressed	General Stroessner in power since 1954.
PERU	Civilian/Parliament 1980	Amnesty in 1979, followed by many arrests	Frequent — as result of action by security forces	Under Attack.	Military regimes 1968-80.
TRINIDAD & TOBAGO	Civilian/Parliament 1967			Legal	Occasional use of army to suppress strikers.
URUGUAY	Military Dictatorship 1973	2,000 (1979) At least 8,000 since 1971	32 known deaths under torture.	Repressed	c. 300,000 people left country 1966-76.
VENEZUELA	Civilian/Parliament 1978	180 in 1979, most released in amnesty.		Legal	

* Military take power in coup, 17 July 1980. Many deaths and arrests reported following popular resistance.

(Amnesty International and various human rights and solidarity committees.)

THREE VIEWS OF GUATEMALA

1. 'GUATEXPRO' (GOVERNMENT EXPORT AGENCY)

Make the Right Investment: Get to Know Guatemala

Just two and one-half hours from New Orleans, in the heart of Central America, a new American frontier has been opened. Both aggressive multinational corporations and lone entrepreneurs have discerned the path of progress into the future and discovered that it leads to Guatemala. In the vernacular . . . the country is 'busting wide open'!

There are excellent reasons why Guatemala is the most highly-favoured site for new investment right now — political and economic stability, resources, modern support facilities . . . a unique and exciting spirit permeates everything we have to say about our country and the opportunities here for you — opportunities that may never occur again.

2. AMNESTY INTERNATIONAL. HUMAN RIGHTS IN GUATEMALA OCT. 1978

Oct. 4th Gonzalo Ac Bin, a member of the consultative council in the ACRICASA trade union (Japanese-owned acrilics manufacturer) is murdered, allegedly by the *policia judicial* (judicial police).

5th Miguel Angel Ordonez, union leader in the CAVISA glass factory shot and killed by police during a demonstration.

7th Arnulfo Cifuentes Diaz, former president of the ARTG (telegraphists union) is shot and killed outside his home. The legal recognition of ARTG is cancelled by the regime in retaliation for the active role it played in mass protests against official plans to raise the costs of public transport by 100%. Other unions have also lost their legal status.

12th Attempt on the life of Rene de Leon Schlotter, agrarian lawyer and Christian Democrat leader, in which his driver dies. Police are on the scene but take no evidence.

18th The ESA (Secret Anti-Communist Army) issues a list of 38 people including trade union, peasant and student leaders as well as church figures, politicians and journalists, whom they have tried and sentenced to death. Several have since been killed but according to AI's understanding government officials have refused to protect those threatened.

20th Oliverio Castaneda, president of the University Student Assoc., is murdered moments after he had spoken at a Revolution Day Rally and in full view of numerous police detachments, which had been controlling the crowds at the rally.

3. INTERNATIONAL NICKEL COMPANY EXECUTIVE 1973

The military will continue to rule in Guatemala for the foreseeable future . . . It is the only base of stability, really. It will rule even with a civilian government in power . . . one of the best prospects in terms of foreign investment.

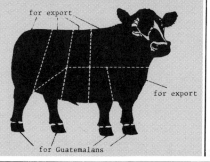

for export

for export

for Guatemalans

labour codes. In fact, the codes have not so much been revised as entirely replaced and the new versions simply legalise the suppression of all effective means of worker organisation.

In all the countries of the Southern Cone of Latin America independent union federations have been outlawed, usually to be replaced by pro-government or 'yellow' organisations. In line with this, regional, national and even industry-wide union structures have been declared illegal. The closed shop is prohibited and 'political activity' on the part of the unions totally banned. In Uruguay the labour code presented for 'discussion' in May 1979 stipulates that all workers standing for union elections must sign a 'declaration of democratic faith' i.e. agree with the policies of the military junta. This is already implemented in the public sector unions.

As in Brazil, Argentina and Chile, the Uruguayan regime has prohibited all strikes in the public sector and 'strategic industries' — a term that is given the widest possible meaning. In Chile, for example, all copper workers are employees in a 'strategic industry'. In Uruguay all unions must present a complete list of their members and full reports of their activities, as well as their accounts, to the authorities at regular intervals. Voting by secret ballot for trade union posts is compulsory and anybody failing to vote is suspended from membership for a year. In Argentina the extensive social security facilities built up by the unions since the late 1940s have been taken over by the military. In Brazil the traditional right to full job security after ten years in employment has been removed and leaders of 'illegal' strikes are subject to prosecution under the decrees of internal security.

The new labour code proposed in Guatemala offers the extension of post-natal leave for women and an extra week's holiday (from two to three) a year for all workers as a concession to the increasingly militant labour movement. But apart from these clauses the measure is a direct attack on the unions. The government has given itself greater judicial powers to disband unions and prevent the formation of new ones if these have, in the eyes of the regime, 'intervened in electoral politics or the affairs of political parties, maintained activities antagonistic to the democratic Constitution' or 'put themselves at the services of foreign interests contrary to those of Guatemala'. Local branches are to be dissolved if they cannot show a membership of at least 20 within 15 days. Strikes by rural workers are banned at harvest time, which is very often the only time they can be sure of employment and certainly the only time when strike action could have any real effect.

MAIN PROPOSALS OF THE CHILEAN LABOUR CODE (DECREED JUNE 1979)

Automatic inclusion of workers into a union forbidden; up to ten different unions permitted in any one workplace.

★ Industry-wide federations are permitted but have no powers whatsoever: bargaining can only be conducted at plant level and no body other than the plant union can participate.

★ Federation dues cannot be deducted from pay.

★ Assemblies can only be outside of worktime.

★ Nomination for union elections is forbidden before the voting day.

★ Trade union leaders are prohibited from participating in any 'political' activity at all; their time off work to conduct union affairs will be severely limited.

★ No employer can contribute to union funds.

★ Any group of workers, unionised or not, may deal with the employer directly; negotiation with third parties is prohibited.

★ All 'acquired rights' are nullified once bargaining starts. Offers cannot be lower than current wages but all conditions and benefits won in earlier contracts are null and void and must be renegotiated from scratch or abandoned altogether if they fall outside 'negotiable' categories.

★ Arbitration in disputes will be by officials appointed by the Junta; no intermediate ruling is allowed.

★ Discussion of 'non-wage benefits' (health, housing, education or job training) are expressly excluded from the bargaining process.

★ All state employees and those who work in 'strategic' industries are forbidden to strike (this applies to all copper workers amongst others).

★ Strikes may last no more than sixty days. At the end of this period workers must either return to work (accepting wages and conditions as they were before) or resign. After thirty days any strikers may desert their fellow workers and negotiate individual contracts. At any time during a strike 10% of the participants can vote to censure the strike leaders and propose the election of a new negotiating team. Workers may not renegotiate to recuperate pay lost during strikes and all those who strike must make their own social security payments.

★ Management has full rights to take on blackleg labour and plants may be closed for the first thirty days of a strike.

12 February 1980—Salvadorean troops arrest wounded demonstrators.

Other proposed changes include a provision for obligatory overtime shifts of up to four hours, as long as the employer states this in contracts, and a clause which makes it a crime to 'incite' a strike either publicly or privately if the stoppage has not already been authorised by the government.

The Unions Under Attack

It has been obvious from the very beginning that the new organisations set up by the dictatorships to replace the independent unions can in no way serve the interests of the workers; they cannot be called authentic trade unions. Quite apart from the fact that they have been imposed upon the labour movement through violence, they have done nothing to improve workers' standards of living; even if they were prepared to do something, they lack any effective power. In Chile the government-appointed union bureaucrats have made some gestures of complaint about the desperate economic situation of the working class, but in order to make any impression they have had to enter into limited cooperation with the independent (and illegal) unions. In Uruguay the pro-government CGTU has done nothing to stop the fall in real wages. It is not surprising, then, that these organisations completely lack mass support.

However, the setting up of pro-government substitutes for national union confederations has not always met with success. In Argentine, despite the fact that the independent union body CUTA has been outlawed, the government has not been able to set up a parallel structure and has relied instead on direct military control of the major unions.

Elsewhere the suppression, intervention or takeover of union offices by government officials, or the setting up of parallel organisations in certain sectors is widespread. Under the military dictatorship of General Banzer the powerful Bolivian miners' union, FSTMB, was banned for a long time and many of its leaders exiled, jailed and even killed. The remaining members of the national leadership had to work underground and the union held a full national congress in secret in 1976. During the attempted coup of November 1979, the military blew up the building that houses the FSTMB and the Bolivian TUC (COB), killing several union employees.

In El Salvador rural unions

Members of the Peruvian teachers' union, SUTEP, at a rally during the 1978 strike.

were declared illegal in 1932 and have remained so for the last 48 years. In general, however, it is more common for unions to be outlawed or intervened only when they prove to be too militant to be controlled by other, less obvious, means. Thus the Ecuadorian teachers union, UNE, which had become increasingly militant, was dissolved by decree, the national leadership arrested, and pay to the entire profession withheld when a national strike was called in May 1977 in support of wage rises, the nationalisation of oil and the removal of anti-worker legislation. UNE has now been given back its legal status. Its Peruvian counterpart — SUTEP — had to fight for several years before it received legal recognition, despite the fact that it is the largest union in the country, because of its consistently militant activity in recent years.

'Yellow union' is the term used in Latin America for unions which collaborate with employers and the government against the interests of their members. Yellow unionism flourishes in Latin America because of a tradition of state patronage and intervention that has always been far stronger and more extensive than in Europe. The most outstanding example of this phenomenon in the Mexican CTM, the entire history of which has been marked by a singular lack of independence from the ruling PRI party and a concentration of power in the hands of the union bureaucracy.

The weakness of the Brazilian labour movement can also be explained as much by the work of the 'pelegos' — pro-government bureaucrats whose background in the unions and appearance of independence has made compliance with the labour code all the more

INDUSTRIAL RELATIONS IN ECUADOR

GOVERNMENT DECREE NO. 1476 OF MAY 1977

The Supreme Council of Government, Considering

That education being one of the most transcendental values in the life of the country, the State, with the desire to encourage its development, assisted the establishment of the National Union of Teachers (UNE);

That it is an obligation for UNE to strengthen and affirm the spirit of national unity and ensure that forces foreign to education do not act against the principles that determine the life of the Republic;

That UNE has not fulfilled its objectives of stimulating and exalting professional responsibility and consciousness, dedicating itself instead to activities contrary to the interests of national education which have advanced the destruction of the principles of authority, order and discipline; and

That it is the duty of the State to oversee the proper progress of education and suppress those organisms that conspire against the integral development of Ecuadorean childhood and youth;

In Using the Powers with which it has been Invested, Decrees:

Article 1: The Ministerial Accord No. 1767 of 15 November 1968 by which the statues of UNE were approved be revoked.

Article 2: The accounts which UNE maintained in keeping with its juridical status be intervened and a complete audit be undertaken.

Article 3: All dispositions which are opposed to the present decree be revoked. The present act is valid as of now.

Article 4: The execution of this decree be put in the charge of the Secretaries of State in the Ministries of Government and Public Education.

Given, in the National Palace, Quito, on 25 May 1977.

Signed
Vice Admiral Alfredo Poveda Burbano
Commander in Chief of the Navy, President of the Supreme Council of Government.

Brigadier General Guillermo Duran A.
Commander in Chief of Land Forces, Member of the Supreme Council of Government.

Brigadier General Luis Leoro Franco
Commander in Chief of the Air Force, Member of the Supreme Council of Government.

Staff Colonel Bolivar N. Jarrin, C.
Minister of Government.

Brigadier General Fernando Dobronsky O.
Minister of Public Education.

effective — as by outright repression. In the case of Brazil the yellow leadership has proved to be especially damaging because of the vertical organisation of the unions which means that all major decisions come from the top.

This system was extended further still by the work of ORIT (Inter-American Regional Organisation of Labour) and the US labour agencies (See **International Organisations**). One of the most glaring examples is the Dominican Republic where the extensive work carried out by the US labour bureaucracy after the invasion by US marines in 1965 led to the establishment of an entire yellow union apparatus which still maintains considerable influence and actively impedes the setting up of new unions and branches.

Almost all the national confederations affiliated to ORIT have a consistently yellow record although it may be that the union leaderships have not been in the pay of governments or even directly organised by them. Nevertheless, government support for the leadership has meant that attempts by rank and file movements to break from the bureaucracy and establish an independent programme have inevitably failed and led to the setting up of separate organisations: thus the price paid for yellow leaderships is not only collabor-

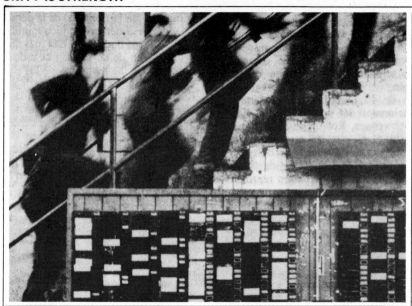

FORD IN ARGENTINA

At Ford's, a plant which is now without any type of union organisation, the superexploitation and persecution of the workers is particularly brutal. Workers throughout the factory are agitating for higher wages; some sections through petitions, others by direct demands to the supervisors for a 50% increase and the raising of the minimum wage from 700,000 to five million pesos.

In the face of this movement management announced that they were considering increases but wouldn't stipulate the amount. At the same time they launched a series of anti-worker measures. First they accelerated the already rapid pace of production on the line and then produced another 'modification' with the extension of the working day. This had already been extended by an extra compulsory hour (from 8 to 9 a day) and has now been lengthened by another hour for the late shift (10 hours a day). In order to force these measures through the management have resorted to threats and intimidations: anybody who doesn't work the new hours will be fired. Apart from the sheer physical effort involved there is an additional setback for comrades who clock in at 4pm because they will now finish work at 2am when there is no transport to take them home.

This bred widespread discontent and the workers were showing open opposition when the bosses announced the details of the pay rises: 15% and no alteration in the minimum.

The management has embarked on a course of deliberate provocation and the indignation of the comrades was plain for all to see. In many sections groups were formed spontaneously to boycott the new regime and return to the eight-hour shift. The comrades refused to comply with the compulsory 'extras'. Through the foremen the management threatened all those who didn't conform but even so a large number of us worked only the normal shift. The next day ten were sacked and eventually this number increased to over fifty. Most of those sacked were known as activists. By the end of the week the whole factory was complying with all the 'extras'.

The company has been able to do this because the workers are not organised and it is almost inevitable that without a union the comrades respond to attacks like this in actions that are spontaneous and desperate. But, although we have suffered a setback, one important effect is that there is now a debate amongst the activists over how to respond to such provocations.

It is clear that the more active comrades must organise ourselves into commissions by section and that these have to be coordinated so that we can develop a strategy for the defence of our wages and the reorganisation of the union in the plant!

Politica Obrera, Argentina, June 1979.

ationist policies but also division. In Chile and Brazil, withdrawal to form independent organisations would lead to extreme isolation and vulnerability. The mass of the workers still belong to these unions and so they remain the logical place in which to build up resistance. In Argentina, where a slightly greater degree of independence exists, this is even more the case.

The Fight Back

While the Latin American labour movement has undoubtedly suffered severe setbacks in recent years, it has continued to fight back, even under the most adverse conditions. In one notable case — Nicaragua — it has made an enormous advance following the overthrow in 1979 of the brutal 40 year-old Somoza dictatorship by the Sandinistas. The freedoms gained by Nicaraguan workers have had an impact in the world at large but they have provided a particularly important example for their comrades in Central America.

The effects are to be seen in the strength of the mass mobilisation in El Salvador, the growing militancy of workers in Honduras, and the resistance to the dictatorship in Guatemala. Even Costa Rica and Panama have felt the impact, with increased pressure on the civilian regimes from the labour movement.

Cuba has for the last 20 years been a socialist state which, in spite of the bureaucratic methods of the government and suppression of independent worker organisation, represents a real advance from the in-built exploitation of the capitalist states in the region. Through the 1959 Revolution Cuban workers have gained the best educational, health and working conditions in the subcontinent. The revolutions in Cuba and Nicaragua have a strong influence in the rest of Latin America and are powerful examples of what can be achieved. There have been others, however, which promised to be of equal magnitude and were subsequently reversed.

The gains made by the workers and peasants of Mexico and Bolivia through the revolutions of 1910-20 and 1952 respectively were at the time considerable but they have since been either eroded and institutionalised, as in Mexico, or stamped out by military dictatorship, as in Bolivia. Today the Mexican working class is weak in organisation and lacking a strong political alternative, but in Bolivia the last two years have witnessed a rapid upturn in labour mobilisation with the miners at the head. This was evident in the stubborn resistance that workers and peasants put up against the coup of the right wing Colonel Natusch in November 1979. Over 200 died in the fortnight of street fighting and strikes that followed Natusch's coup, but the regime

TWO VIEWS ON INDUSTRIAL PEACE IN BRAZIL

1. 'BRAZILIAN TRENDS' (SAO PAULO, APRIL 1973)

The labour legislation passed in 1964 drastically reduced the number of industrial conflicts. In Sao Paulo, the country's largest industrial centre, the number of strikes fell from 302 in 1963 to *none* in 1971 . . . Meanwhile in the more advanced countries the number of hours lost through work stoppages is growing amazingly: in Italy 250 million work hours were lost in 1970, three times more than in 1963; in England, the 5,000 strikes in 1971 absorbed 13.5 million working hours . . . in the US just the 1970 General Motors strike involving 400,000 workers cost the country $1 billion and the firm $220 million in profits.

2. MANOEL DA CONCEICAO, LEADER OF THE RURAL WORKERS UNION OF VALE DO PINDARE
(A letter smuggled out of a prison in Rio de Janiero, Dec. 1972. It is not known if he is still alive)

I spent four months facing heavy torture in the 1st Army Barracks of Rio de Janiero and later in the Navy Secret Service — CENIMAR . . . They tore out my fingernails. They perforated my penis and my testicles until they came to resemble a sieve. They tied a rope to my testicles and dragged me on the terrace, then hung me upside down. They chained my wrists and hung me on a bar, took off my artificial leg and tied up my penis so I couldn't urinate. They left me without food and drink and on only one leg. They gave me so many electric shocks that my eardrums burst and I am impotent.

They nailed my penis to a table and left me nailed for 24 hours. They threw me in a pool, tied up like a pig; I almost drowned. They put me in a cell that was almost completely dark. I spent 28 days urinating and defecating in the same place where I lay down to sleep . . . They put me inside a rubber box, turned on a horn so that for eight days I didn't eat or sleep and I almost went crazy. They injected my blood stream with 'truth serum' . . . They lay me down on the floor and threatened to tear out my guts through my rectum . . .

Industrial peace in Brazil.

LABOUR STRUGGLES IN PERU 1978

Jan. 24th State of emergency declared in Chimbote after 48-hour general strike and seven week stoppage in the state steel mill.

Feb. 27th- 28th General strike called by CGTP receives support of 70% of workers in Lima and paralyses industry in the capital. Government gives mayors powers to rule on legality of strikes and order their repression.

Mar. 23rd New labour laws published. Clauses include extension of number of reasons for dismissal outside the workplace and the admissibility of police reports as evidence for dismissal. Wave of protest strikes includes a general strike in the city of Arequipa.

May 8th National strike by national teachers' union SUTEP begins.

May 19th Increases of 50-60% in food prices decreed in compliance with IMF requirements. State of emergency declared; 50 parliamentary candidates arrested.

May 22nd- 23rd General strike called by CGTP and CNT halts all activity in Lima. 90% of workers answer call. A curfew is imposed and five die in demonstrations in the capital. There are also demonstrations in Cuzco, Huanuco and Arequipa where an eight day general strike takes place and over 21 people are shot by police.

Aug. 4th- Sept 6th National miners' strike. Government declares stoppage illegal and gives workers three days to return to work or lose their jobs. 10,000 miners march to Lima to demand the release of over 200 union leaders arrested in previous 18 months. Five mining areas placed under military rule. Clerical staff at the US-owned Southern Peru Copper Co. come out in sympathy. 7,000 railwaymen on the Cuzco-Arequipa line work to rule. State shipworkers, bankworkers, and civil servants come out. Miners denounced as 'wreckers' by the dailies *El Peruano* and *La Cronica* the journalists of which themselves strike for better pay, union recognition and guarantees of job security.

Wreckage in the Bolivian TUC (COB) and the Mineworkers' Union (FSTMB) building after bombing during the November '79 coup attempt.

was finally overthrown principally due to the action of the working class following a general strike and the complete closedown of the mines. This action, born of widespread awareness of the political interests of the working class, has been consolidated by the continuing mobilisation of the unions, with increasing participation by the peasants, over economic demands. The level of trade union and political activity in the country is now greater than it has been at any time in the last decade.

In Peru there has been a notable increase in unrest in the last two years which provided a major setback for the 12 year-old military regime. The main impetus for this challenge came from the IMF's demands for major cuts in public expenditure which made the impact of the economic crisis on the poor even worse. The military responded with increasingly violent measures but despite the fragmentation within the Peruvian labour movement much of the impetus of the strikes of 1978 and 1979 has been maintained. As the army hands over power to the new civilian government, having failed to provide the 'peace and order' it proclaimed as its prime objectives, the unions will necessarily become increasingly involved in a political struggle in order to defend the standard of living of their members.

If the gains made by the labour movement under the harshest dictatorships have been slight compared to those elsewhere in Latin America, they are nevertheless impressive. In Guatemala the two major federations and over 160 unions, as well as more than 150 peasant organisations, have formed the Democratic Front Against Repression in defence of basic democratic rights. In view of the failure of opposition political parties to survive repression by the military, the unions now offer the only substantial resistance which promises to develop into a major challenge, especially since the success of the sugar workers' strike early in 1980 (See **PART TWO**).

Seven years after the coup in Chile the last two May Days have been celebrated with demonstrations in Santiago — at the cost of scores of arrests —

Chile—2000 turn out for the 'illegal' May Day parade in '79.

which, under the circumstances, was a massive show of solidarity. A month later a railway strike paralysed transport around Buenos Aires. Earlier in the year demands for a 50% wage increase in the Renault plant led to a stoppage by 10,000 workers. Power, rail, maritime and bank workers have all come out on strike since the coup in March 1976. The traditionally militant car workers have, however, been unable to move beyond isolated actions because of the military intervention of the metal workers union SMATA and the particularly high level of repression in this sector. Nevertheless, the fact that the government has been forced to negotiate with the 'illegal' CUTA and that CUTA itself has come under pressure from its own members to call a general strike against the labour code shows that there is a definite revival within the union movement.

An even stronger resurgence has taken place in Brazil, which is all the more surprising in view of the country's history of yellow unionism: the emergence of the *Oposicao Sindical* (Union Opposition) movement based amongst the metal and car workers of Sao Paulo. The strikes led by this broad move-

ment in 1978 and 1979 were the first major show of strength by Brazilian workers in ten years and certainly the greatest challenge to the regime from the labour movement since the 1964 coup. The *Oposicao Sindical* has not limited itself to economic demands but has attacked the union bureaucracy, the labour code and the government. This has exposed it to repression but on several occasions support for stoppages has been so great that the dictatorships has held back for fear of setting off riots in the large industrial cities.

Even in Panama, where the labour movement is small and has had a long history of division, a general strike on 28-29 January 1980 brought the capital city, the banana and oil industries and most of the Canal Zone to a halt as unions protested at changes in labour laws which encouraged private investment, eroded workers' rights and reduced job security.

This renewal of union activity in several Latin American countries has, of course, been determined by widely varying political conditions but the trend is unmistakeable. Under these circumstances international solidarity can be particularly effective.

and the rank and file of the major unions have openly rejected the labour code even though, as in the case of the copper workers, their leadership is government appointed. Small but persistent signs of resistance such as the boycotting of canteens and the spoiling of ballot papers have shown a rising spirit of combativity. The illegal strike by the entire 11,000 workforce of the El Teniente copper mine in January 1980 is evidence of a significant advance in the resistance of the Chilean workers.

In Argentina a step of equal significance was taken with the calling of a 'national day of protest' (the word 'strike' is illegal) in late April 1979 which drew the support of 30% of workers in the major cities

Brazil's metalworkers assemble during the March '79 strike. Fernando Ochoa

INTERNATIONAL TRADE UNION ORGANISATIONS

The vast majority of workers throughout the world are unaware of the existence of the international trade union organisations. This clearly demonstrates their failure to develop effective international solidarity. This failure stems less from difficulties in organisation than from political bias, for there is no such thing as impartial and apolitical worker solidarity.

One of the key issues with regard to the trade union internationals is the degree to which they take a forthright stand in practice against 'imperialism' — that is, not just the multinational corporations but also their political interests, which are most often identified with the policies of the US government and its

Working for Ford—
Swansea and Sao Paulo—divided and ruled.

leading allies.

There are certainly political differences of substance between the main organisations but these are not as great as they themselves claim. What is more important is that none of them has proved capable of responding to the needs of rank and file workers in Latin America. In many places their existence affects only the local union bureaucracy, and there is an increasing trend for trade unionists committed to an independent labour movement to reject affiliation to these organisations and to discuss alternative forms of regional coordination.

One of the main ways in which workers in the western industrialised countries can further the struggle of those in the neo-colonial world is to intervene in these international organisations and fight for them to become instruments of a truly independent working class internationalism.

World Federation of Trade Unions (WFTU)

Founded 1945.

Headquarters: Vinohradska 10, Prague 2, Czechoslovakia.

British office: 103a, Hoe St., London E17 4SA.

Claims 70 member organisations, representing 150 million workers in 68 countries.

Latin American affiliate: CPUSTAL (Congreso Permanente de Unidad Sindical de los Trabajadores de America Latina/ Permanent Congress of Trade Union Unity of Latin American Workers). Based in Mexico City. CPUSTAL was established in 1964. Through its membership of the WFTU, CPUSTAL is identified with the interests of the Soviet Bloc and attacked for its 'communism', but on several occasions it has attempted, without success, to collaborate with the other regional trade union organisations. Apart from Cuba, which continues to be

its main backer, the principal base of CPUSTAL was in the Chilean CUT, but since the coup this has been all but destroyed.

Despite the fact that CPUSTAL is much the most consistent of all the organisations in issuing anti-imperialist rhetoric, its record has not been revolutionary in practice. Its reliance upon Soviet backing has meant that its influence largely depends on the strength of the local Communist parties and its work has followed their policies. Hence, CPUSTAL has had to contend with the CP's belief in the existence of a broad anti-imperialist and democratic sector of the Latin American capitalist class which has weakened its capacity to provide adequate leadership in the fight against dictatorship. The result has been that the CPs in Latin America, which are in any case small and of limited political significance in most countries, have failed to grow and this is mirrored in CPUSTAL itself. Moreover,

CPUSTAL is attacked from right and left alike for the suppression of independent workers' organisations in Cuba.

World Confederation of Labour (WCL)

Founded in 1920 as the International Confederation of Christian Trade Unions; took its current name in 1968.

Headquarters: 26, Rue Juste Lipse, Brussels 4, Belgium.

Claims 90 member organisations, representing 25 million workers in 72 countries.

Latin American affiliate: CLAT (Central Latinoamericana de Trabajadores/Latin American Confederation of Workers. Based in Caracas, Venezuela. CLAT was founded in 1961 along the WCL guidelines of promoting a 'third way' for the working class between communism and capitalism. It is certainly true that CLAT is equally virulent in its attacks on CPUSTAL and ORIT — the regional organisation of the ICFTU (see below) — which it sees as opposed to the

'liberation of the people from imperialism'. Nevertheless, CLAT's own record falls far short of the claims made in its radical statements and literature. It receives the great bulk of its funds from Christian Democratic foundations in Europe that are clearly not 'anti-imperialist' in any way, and these funds are rigorously controlled by the central bureaucracy in Caracas, for its own political purposes.

The leadership of the Ecuadorian Confederation of Class Organisations (CEDOC), once affiliated to CLAT, claims that CLAT has strong links with the CIA in Ecuador and that it is determined to further its own political interest there at the expense of a unified and radical workers' movement. Similar charges have been levelled by the National Confederation of Workers (CNT) in Guatemala, which disaffiliated when CLAT tried to stop it from participating in the Confederation for Trade Union Unity (CNUS) which is working to bring together all the workers' organisations in the struggle against the military regime. The Honduran General Confederation of Workers (CGT) came close to leaving when CLAT demanded that 25% of all funds received by the CGT from abroad be sent to Caracas, a demand that has since been dropped.

CLAT also suffers from its close attachment to the politics of Christian Democracy in Latin America which have consistently shown themselves in practice to contradict CLAT's stated aims. While the organisation benefitted from its outspoken opposition to ORIT, it is clear that the movement against CLAT is growing, most particularly among those unions that were formerly members.

International Confederation of Free Trade Unions (ICFTU)

Founded in 1949 in a split from the WFTU.

Headquarters: Rue Montagne-aux-Herbes-Potageres 37-41, B-1000, Brussels, Belgium.

British office: TUC.

Claims 118 affiliated organisations, representing 60 million workers in 96 countries.

American regional organisation: ORIT (Organizacion Regional Inter-Americana del Trabajo/Inter-American Regional Organisation of Labour). Based in Mexico City.

From its formation in 1951, ORIT has been under the

influence of the American AFL-CIO (American Federation of Labour-Congress of Industrial Organisations) which, along with the AIFLD (American Institute for Free Labour Development), has moulded it into a resolutely pro-US body, lacking any real financial, organisational or political independence.

When the AFL-CIO left the ICFTU in the late 1960s, because the European social democrats had 'gone soft' on communism, the ICFTU stopped funding ORIT but it still retains formal links with the organisation. Although the TUC and ICFTU leadership have consequently played down their association with ORIT, they still claim that there is no evidence that ORIT has participated in CIA-backed operations and deny that it is little more than an instrument for US interests in Latin America.

The failure of the ICFTU to condemn ORIT is of the utmost importance for British workers. In effect, it puts them, through the TUC, in the same camp as an organisation which was expelled from Bolivia in 1969 for 'acting openly in the interests of imperialism', repudiated by the Argentine CGT on the same grounds and bitterly denounced in Chile, Guyana, Guatemala, Brazil and the Dominican Republic for its support of right wing regimes, military coups and US invasion.

Many ORIT affiliates still support dictatorial regimes and it is only recently that the ICFIU has begun to expel such organisations, notably the Salvadorean CGS, the CPT in Paraguay and the CTF in Guatemala. Nothing, however, has been done about ORIT. There is no doubt that it remains an acute embarrassment and some ICFTU affiliates have pressed for something to be done about ORIT, but there is no ready alternative.

The case of ORIT is not an exception in the history of the ICFTU: it is the direct result of a general policy of encouraging 'free and democratic unions' in the Third World modelled on those in the capitalist states of western Europe. The ICFTU's aim that such unions should be 'apolitical' and yet at the same time staunchly anti-communist is not only an absurd contradiction but also quite unworkable, particularly in the neo-colonial world. In the context of Latin America, 'freedom' and 'democracy' have clearly tended to mean support for US policies and US control.

The American Institute for Free Labour Development (AIFLD)

Founded in 1961 at the suggestion of George Meany, president of the AFL-CIO for 36 years, the AIFLD has been the main vehicle for US labour policy in Latin America and the

Breaking of the chains.

Women in Struggle—political demonstration in Ecuador.

that area. Our collaboration takes the form of trying to make the investment climate more attractive and more inviting to them'. To this end AIFLD has 'trained' over 200,000 Latin American trade unionists, many of them in its 'graduate school' in Virginia. Before the coup in Chile it offered its guidance to nearly 9,000 union leaders, centering its attention on the maritime workers union which played a direct part in bringing about the overthrow of Allende.

Chilean truck owners' strike backed by the CIA to overthrow Popular Unity.

principal influence on the direction of ORIT. The AIFLD receives some funds from the AFL-CIO but much the largest share of its budget comes from the US government and corporations, representatives of which sit on its board of directors. Among the companies which have made donations to the AIFLD are W.R.Grace, Rockefeller, ITT, Kennecott, First National City Bank, Mobil Oil, Anaconda and United Fruit — corporations that are renowned for their long histories of exploitation and political intervention in Latin America.

In 1969 the AIFLD executive director declared: 'We are collaborating with the Council on Latin America which is made up of the primary US business institutions that have activities in

It is not surprising that one political weekly has said, 'No self-respecting journalist would refer to AIFLD without in the next breath making some reference to the CIA'. In his book *CIA Diary* Philip Agee recounts how, as an agent in Latin America, he worked with the AIFLD. Executive director William Doherty openly boasted to a US Senate enquiry in 1968 about the organisation's role in the right wing coup in Brazil in 1964: 'What happened in Brazil did not just happen, it was planned, and months in advance. Many of the trade union leaders, some of whom were trained in our own institute, were involved'.

The International Trade Secretariats (ITSs)

The ITSs are autonomous confederations of unions in the

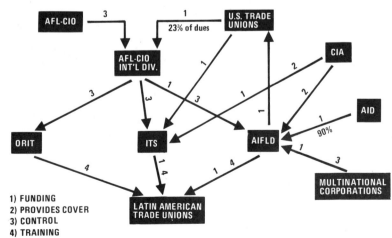

1) FUNDING
2) PROVIDES COVER
3) CONTROL
4) TRAINING

same industry or occupation. They are European in origin and mostly grouped around the ICFTU but because of the strong US presence in the Latin American work of the ITSs they came to be dominated by the AFL-CIO and AIFLD; they have become instruments of their policy, funded by them and staffed by their appointees.

As early as 1962 AIFLD board member George Lodge wrote: 'ITS flexibility, inner cohesion and conviction makes the Secretariats especially effective anti-communist instruments in the so-called neutralist areas and they are extremely important to US objectives'.

The Retail Clerks International channelled CIA money for the overthrow of the progressive Jagan government in Guyana in 1963; the International Federation of Petroleum and Chemical Workers was funded by the CIA for operations in Brazil and was eventually expelled from the country by the military dictatorship! In Chile the International Transport Workers Federation played a leading role in organising reactionary strikes against the Allende government and was involved in paving the way for the 1973 coup.

This US control over ITS operations in Latin America has been resisted by the European headquarters, but with only limited success and very few of them have an acceptable record. Amongst those that have shown themselves prepared to undertake genuine solidarity work are the miners (MIF) and food-workers (IUF), but even these suffer badly from lack of finance and support from a membership which is almost entirely ignorant of their existence.

Industry-based solidarity work is especially effective but the great potential strength of the ITSs can only be realised through far greater worker participation and control.

INTERNATIONAL TRADE SECRETARIATS

Miners' International Federation (MIF)
Peter Tait, General Secretary
75-76 Blackfriars Road
London SE1 8HE
Great Britain
Membership: 1,269,825 (31.12.1973)

International Metalworkers' Federation (IMF)
Herman Rebhan, General Secretary
Routes des Acacias
54 bis — Case Postale 325
CH-1227 Carouge-Geneva
Switzerland
Membership: 13,000,000(31.12.1975)

International Graphical Federation
Heinz Coke, International Secretary
Monbijoustrasse, 73
CH-3007 Bern
Switzerland
Membership: 835,386 (31.12.1974)

International Federation of Chemical Energy and General Workers' Unions (ICF)
Charles Levinson, General Secretary
58 rue de Moillebeau
CH-1211 — Geneva 19
Switzerland
Membership: 6,000,000 (29.10.1976)

International Union of Food and Allied Workers' Associations (IUF)
Dan Gallin, General Secretary
Rampe du Pont-Rouge 8
CH-1213 Petit-Lancy
Switzerland
Membership: 2,152,077 (31.12.1973)

Universal Alliance of Diamond Workers
Albert Buelens, General Secretary
Plantin-en-Moretuslei, 66-68
B-2000 Antwerpen
Belgium
Membership: 10,880 (31.12.1971)

International Textile, Garment and Leather Workers' Federation (ITGLWF)
Charles Ford, General Secretary
Rue Joseph Stevens, 8
B-1000 Brussels
Belgium
Membership: 4,800,000 (31.12.1973)

Public Services International (PSI)
Carl. W.Franken, General Secretary
Hallstrom House
Central Way
Feltham (Middlesex)
Great Britain
Membership: 4,131,944 (31.12.1972)

International Federation of Plantation, Agricultural and Allied Workers (IFPAAW)
Stanley G.Correa, General Secretary
17 rue Necker
CH-1201 Geneva
Switzerland
Membership: 1,400,000 (31.12.1975)

International Transport Workers Federation (ITWF)
Harold Lewis, General Secretary
Maritime House
Old Town, Clapham
London SW4 0JR
Great Britain
Membership: 5,000,000 (31.12.1973)

International Federation of Free Teachers' Unions (IFFTU)
Andre Braconier, General Secretary
Avenue Bergmann, 111
1050 Brussels
Belgium
Membership: 1,200,000 (31.12.1971)

Postal, Telegraph and Telephone International (PTTI)
Stefan Nedzynski, General Secretary
36 avenue du Lignon
CH-1219 Le Lignon-Geneva
Switzerland
Membership: 3,246,417 (1.7.1975)

International Secretariat of Entertainment Trade Unions (ISETU)
J.Schweinzer, President
c/o Gewerkschaft Kunst, Medien, Freie Berufe
Maria-Theresien Strasse, 11
A-1090 Wien
Austria
Membership: 492,741 (31.12.1975)

International Federation of Commercial Clerical and Technical Employees (FIET)
Heribert Maier, General Secretary
15 avenue de Balexert
CH-1211 Geneva 28
Switzerland
Membership: 6,000,000 (1.7.1975)

International Federation of Building and Woodworkers (IFBWW)
John E.Lofbad, General Secretary
27-29 rue de la Coulouvreniere
CH-1204 Geneva
Switzerland
Membership: 3,000,000 (31.12.1974)
(TUC)

SOLIDARITY

The case for the solidarity of British and European workers with their Latin American comrades is overwhelming. Many workers share the same employer, millions work in the same trade and almost all enjoy benefits that have not yet been won in Latin America.

At the level of individual unions perhaps the best record of solidarity is that of the NUM which has twice sent missions to Bolivia, Chile and Peru to investigate the conditions there. It has established strong links with the unions in these countries and published excellent reports on the findings of delegations. Another impressive example is the pressure put on Saab-Scania by its union in Sweden which forced the company to recognise the union in its Brazilian plant in 1977. Similarly, when the Italian metallurgical federation, which includes workers in firms such as Fiat and Olivetti, negotiated collective contracts with employers in 1977 it insisted on a clause that compelled recognition of unions in all the companies' factories throughout the world.

In April 1980 the International Union of Food and Allied Workers' Associations (IUF) launched an international campaign against Coca Cola because of the repression in its Guatemalan plant. This led to a one-day strike by the company's Swedish workers and solidarity action in Australia, Mexico, Spain, Denmark, Norway and Finland. The GMWU has also played an important part in supporting sugar workers in Guyana in recent year. Dockers in Britain and elsewhere have a consistent record of blacking cargoes to and from Latin American countries where workers have been repressed. This does not just apply to Chile — the Dutch dockers blacked Honduran cargoes in

Brazilian dockers load a cargo of coffee to be shipped to Britain. Dockers in Britain have blacked cargoes in solidarity with Latin American workers. USPG

the summer of 1975 following the massacre of peasant union leaders in the Olancho region; shipments of arms to El Salvador and Argentina, amongst others, have been blacked in British ports in the last three years. British dockers play an important role in the Chile Solidarity Campaign.

Direct action of this type is, however, the exception rather than the rule. Moreover, even though they are relatively isolated, Latin American unions in the traditional sectors — miners, railwaymen, dockers, metalworkers — receive more attention than those in white-collar occupations or state employment such as teachers, hospital workers or municipal employees. In 1979 teachers in Brazil, Peru, Bolivia and Panama embarked on major strikes and suffered considerable repression in pursuit of conditions well below those existing in Britain. The SUTEP strikes in Peru got some publicity through an article in *The Teacher* but the others went ignored and unsupported.

At the same time as members of NUPE and COHSE were taking action in demand of a £60 minimum wage in the winter of 1978/9, hospital workers in Costa Rica and Honduras were also striking for better wages and improved conditions but since all these workers are amongst the poorest paid it would have been extraordinarily difficult for them to have undertaken solidarity work alone.

It is, anyway, hard to argue the case for support for cane cutters in Guyana, Coca Cola workers in Guatemala or fishermen in Peru when workers in Britain are faced with a major economic recession. This is particularly the case when a Conservative government is unleashing a well-prepared offensive against the unions, and domestic industry is being run

To General Romeo Lucas Garcia
President of the Republic of Guatemala

We, as representatives of the British trade union movement, are deeply disturbed by the reports we have received from Amnesty International and other organisations of the repression of the trade unions in Guatemala, particularly during the last year and a half. Trade union leaders pursuing their members' legitimate rights as guaranteed by the Guatemalan Labour Code have been the victims of death threats, kidnappings, torture and murder at the hands of clandestine death squads such as the Secret Anti-Communist Army (ESA).

The assassinations of the Coca Cola workers' union leaders, Pedro Quevedo y Quevedo and Manuel Lopez Balam, the killing of Ricardo Martinez Solorzano of the union of workers of the Guatemalan Institute of Social Security and the death, after being kidnapped and brutally tortured, of the journalist Jose Leon Castaneda Juarez, General Secretary of the mass media workers' union SIMCOS, are just four examples of many similar cases where trade unionists in numerous industries have disappeared or been murdered apparently in direct reprisal for their trade union activities. Furthermore, evidence strongly suggests the complicity of government agents in such acts.

We condemn all such acts of repression against the Guatemalan labour movement with which we express our full solidarity. We call upon you and your government to halt these crimes and bring to justice all those responsible.

Guatemala is a signatory to ILO conventions 87 and 98 and therefore pledged to guarantee the most basic trade union freedoms. These conventions have consistently been violated in Guatemala and we insist that measures are taken to ensure their immediate implementation.

Signed:

General Secretary, Transport & General Workers' Union

Secretary, National Union of Mineworkers

President, National Union of Journalists

President, National Union of Mineworkers

General Secretary, National Association of Local Government Officers

January, 1980

down and unemployment rising at such a rate that entire areas of Clydeside, Merseyside, South Wales and the North are facing a depression on a scale not seen since the 1930s.

The media present this as a specifically national crisis and there are some in the labour movement who largely agree with this. Last autumn, for example, Hector Smith of the blastfurnacemen's union argued in *Steel News* that demanning be accepted by workers in British Leyland as it had been up to then in the steel industry so that 'we can knock hell out of our competitors . . . Let us have solidarity — solidarity of purpose, steelmen and carmen. To get this bloody lovely country of ours moving again'.

Such an approach inevitably leads to calls for import controls in defence of the living standard of British workers. This, of course, means solidarity precisely *against* foreign workers on the basis of nationality

CHILE SOLIDARITY CAMPAIGN TRADE UNION CONFERENCE SATURDAY OCTOBER 25 1975

DRAFT DECLARATION

THIS CONFERENCE OF TRADE UNIONISTS

Declares its full support for the struggle of Chilean trade unionists to free themselves from the brutal oppression of a fascist military dictatorship;

Notes that after two years of military rule, repression is still increasing, directly via arbitrary arrest, detention without trial, and torture, and indirectly via economic policies that have more than halved real wages, allowed prices to rocket and thrown hundreds of thousands out of work; that meanwhile all forms of collective bargaining are outlawed, elections to trade union posts are forbidden, and strikers face the death penalty; that thousands of trade unionists are detained without trial, and many have disappeared without trace since their arrest, while others are forced to flee into exile with their families; that DINA, the Chilean Gestapo, has paid informers in every workplace, and operates with complete immunity, responsible only to General Pinochet;

Recognises that it is the Chilean people itself which will overthrow the military junta, by the efforts and organisation of its political parties, its trade union movement, and with the support of all Chileans who oppose fascism;

But reaffirms that international solidarity is indispensable for the struggle of the Chilean people against fascism; only in this way can the military junta be weakened and isolated from its principal sources of support, which are the US government and its agencies, the CIA, the international financiers, ITT and the other multinational corporations of the US, Europe and Japan;

In the conviction that in attacking the resort to fascist methods in Chile, the British labour movement is contributing to its own defence against any similar attempt in Britain.

WE PLEDGE OURSELVES TO WORK:

★ to publicise throughout the British labour movement the truth about events in Chile, through meetings, film shows, pamphlets, articles, leaflets, etc.

Chilean construction workers under Popular Unity government.

★ to secure the freedom of trade union and political prisoners in Chile, through protests, resolutions, delegations and the 'Adopt a Prisoner' campaign.

★ to press the British government to withdraw all forms of support for the Chilean regime.

★ to assist Chilean refugees arriving in Great Britain, and to help them to explain their case to the labour movement.

★ to bring an end to all British trade with or investment in Chile, while such action is requested by the Chilean trade union movement.

★ to respond to the requests for solidarity made by the Central Unica de Trabajadores, the Chilean TUC, which has been banned by the junta.

AT THIS TIME WE MAKE A SPECIAL CALL UPON THE BRITISH GOVERNMENT:

★ to cancel all outstanding arms contracts with the Chilean regime and armed forces, and in particular

to refuse to hand over those submarines, destroyers and aero-engines at present in Britain.

★ to take the lead in the General Assembly of the United Nations to move the condemnation of the Chilean military regime for its persistent violations of human rights, to establish economic sanctions and an embargo on arms sales to the junta by member states.

★ to persist in refusing to renegotiate the Chilean debt, and to take the further steps necessary to make this policy effective, by demanding economic sanctions, including the seizure of Chilean assets in Britain, if payment is not forthcoming.

★ to take measures to secure the supply of copper to Britain from countries other than Chile.

AND UPON THE BRITISH LABOUR MOVEMENT:

★ to give every possible support to the initiative of the executive council of the National Union of Seamen in calling for a boycott of British ships sailing to or from Chile.

★ to support the stand of the Transport & General Workers Union in refusing to allow Rolls-Royce aero-engines to be shipped to Chile.

★ to make every effort to halt the supply of goods, especially machinery, vehicles and chemicals to Chile.

★ to bring every pressure to bear to halt British imports from Chile, especially of copper, nitrates, timber products, wine, fruit, and vegetables, all of which can be easily substituted from other sources.

★ to give positive support to other trade unionists involved in boycott action.

★ to speed up the adoption of Chilean trade union prisoners, which has already helped to secure several releases.

ACHIEVEMENTS SO FAR

★ (November 1973) Liverpool dockers black Chilean ship

★ AUEW workers at Rolls-Royce East Kilbride refuse to service Chilean fighter engines

★ T&GWU Scottish transport workers refuse to move fighter engines

★ Weir Pumps, Cathcart. Pumps for Chilean warships blacked

★ Anderson Mavors, Glasgow. Gearboxes for conveyor belts for Chilean mines blacked

★ GEC Bradford. Switchgear for Chilean submarines blacked

★ STUC and TUC make official consumer boycott of Chilean wine

★ (February 1976) Simultaneous pickets in 14 towns throughout Britain of Ravel shoe shops selling Chilean footwear

★ (September 1975) NUS instructs British seamen not to sail on ships calling at Chilean ports. 600 unemployed seamen in Liverpool refuse to sign up on PSNC ships

★ NUR crane drivers at Newhaven docks refuse to unload Chilean onions. Cargo rots

★ BMC workers refuse to allow export of spares and components to British Leyland factory in Chile

★ ICI Northwich workers resolve to produce nothing more for Chile

★ ITF orders affiliates to commence systematic harassment of Chilean transport from January 1 1976

★ Port workers at Rosyth refuse to service Chilean frigate

★ Workers at Pirelli, Southampton, urge management to obtain copper elsewhere than from Chile

A PEOPLE UNITED WILL NEVER BE DEFEATED!

Chris Welch

BLACKING IS IMPORTANT

The Chilean junta depends on foreign finance and foreign investment; on its ability to import arms and machinery and to export copper, nitrates, timber products, and the vast surplus stocks of food, clothing, shoes and other goods which the Chilean people need, but cannot afford to buy.

Blacking actions took place in Britain within days of the coup itself, and have since been one of the most important contributions of British solidarity. Even partial or temporary blackings have useful effects:

★ they make trade with the junta more expensive and more risky

★ they make British companies hesitate before investing in Chile

★ they set an example to be followed by trade unionists elsewhere and abroad

★ they disrupt the junta's plans, and shake the confidence of its supporters

★ they bring great encouragement to Chilean workers

WHY SOLIDARITY? BRITISH TRADE UNIONISTS SPEAK

In attacking the resort to fascist methods in Chile, the British labour movement is contributing to its own defence against any similar attempt in Britain.

*CSC Trade Union
Conference Declaration*

Our solidarity is no mere charity. For what we can achieve in defence of the workers of a strange and distant country is a powerful demonstration of what a struggle we will wage in our own defence against the same forces that acted in Chile, and which, in more subtle ways, act here — imperialism, the multi-national corporations, and monopoly capital.

*Alex Kitson, in Labour Monthly
January 1976*

I think we have got to review the situation of fascism in the world, not just as a question of what good we can do for the people of Spain, or Chile, or anywhere else . . . but more particularly with regard to the defence of our own position.

Sid Easton, T&GWU Region 1

The engineers in this audience should remember or know that Babcock & Wilcox, British Leyland, EMI, Joseph Lucas, British Ropes, are British based companies which operate in Chile. Bowaters, British American Tobacco, ICI, Lloyds Bank, Shell, Unilever and many others are the same. These companies in which we sweat make profit out of the misery of the Chilean people. But beyond that they gather experience in exploiting a working class, stripped of all legal organisation and expression.

*Harry Smith, National Organiser,
AUEW-TASS*

rather than *with* them on the basis of common class interests. In addition, import controls are likely to invite rapid retaliation. They would, in any case, be of only temporary and partial use since the present crisis, like all major crises, is international in scope.

The British labour movement has shown its potential for internationalism very clearly in its solidarity with Chile. Over 440 delegates representing 34 unions, 35 trades councils and 19 shop stewards committees attended the trade union conference on Chile in October 1975, and the campaigns for boycotts, blacking, adoption of political prisoners and support for refugees show that significant advances can be made.

"COMPETITION IS THE LIFE-BLOOD OF TRADE, FELLOWS, LET'S SEE SOME COMPETITION, LET'S SEE SOME BLOOD!"

This work has to be sustained but it needs to be extended to the rest of Latin America. Equally, it needs to be part of a political campaign since the Conservative government has, within a year of office, cut visas for Latin American refugees, restored ambassadors to Chile and Argentina and adopted a scarcely veiled policy of support for dictatorial regimes.

If solidarity is to be at all effective at an international level it clearly must have the support of the international union confederations as well as that of the trade secretariats. This will require greater openness in the TUC's international work and

Tin miners in Bolivia. The NUM plays an active role in supporting the struggles of these workers. USPG

full discussion in conference so that its record and policies as well as those of the ICFTU are debated and determined democratically within the British labour movement.

At present one of the greatest constraints on solidarity action is the lack of information and proper channels of communication with foreign workers. Yet information about direct company links with Latin America, and other neo-colonial parts of the world, is often to be found on the shopfloor itself. If it is difficult to obtain, branches can request the central union research staff to investigate these links and then establish a monitoring committee.

Union headquarters can also be pressed to contact corresponding unions in Latin America, obtain details of their conditions and requests for support. There is scarcely any industry where this cannot be improved and there are many where it will have to be done from scratch at company as well as industry-wide level.

Obviously conditions vary a good deal; the situation in Panama will be very different to that in Chile, and this emphasises the importance of direct links so that the response can be tailored to specific needs. For example, the NUM was instrumental in stopping a £19 million British government aid package to the Bolivian state mining corporation when asked to do so by the Bolivian miners union, the FSTMB, because of the widespread violation of human rights under the dictatorship of General Hugo Banzer. Later the NUM was asked to campaign for the reestablishment of the aid when, in the summer of 1978, the FSTMB considered that political conditions had improved sufficiently for it to benefit the workers rather than bolster the repressive regime. Only the FSTMB could properly make such a decision and only close collaboration could make it effective.

Specific links of this type are absolutely vital but solidarity also goes beyond this. The most consistent requests from Latin America have been for the raising of issues of democratic and trade union rights violations in

British workers march in solidarity with Chilean workers on the sixth anniversary of the coup—September 1979. CALA

TABLE 3: UNITED KINGDOM TRADE WITH LATIN AMERICA* FOR 1977 AND 1978 BY PRODUCT GROUP

£ THOUSANDS

	UK IMPORTS FROM LATIN AMERICA (cif)		UK EXPORTS TO LATIN AMERICA (fob)	
	1977	1978	1977	1978
Food and live animals	235,838	210,836	17,205	20,461
variation (%)		−10.6		+18.9
Beverages & tobacco	26,509	37,433	64,456	90,456
variation (%)		+41.2		+40.3
Crude materials, inedible except fuels	220,833	228,475	7,358	9,474
variation (%)		+3.5		+28.7
Minerals fuels, lubricants, related materials	56,333	58,115	18,049	7,004
variation (%)		+3.2		−61.2
Animal, vegetable oils and fats	13,174	14,147	882	594
variation (%)		+7.4		−32.7
Chemicals	22,853	29,121	144,369	135,445
variation (%)		+27.4		−6.2
Manufactured goods classified chiefly by material	140,219	138,262	113,129	134,633
variation (%)		−1.4		+19.0
Machinery and transport equipment	33,710	39,823	536,598	481,892
variation (%)		+18.1		−10.2
Miscellaneous manufactured articles	12,707	20,233	45,459	51,466
variation (%)		+59.2		+13.2
Commodities & transactions not classified according to kind	580	2,181	17,091	19,084
variation (%)		+276.0		+11.7
Total	762,755	778,646	964,595	950,509
Variation (%)		+2.1		−1.5

Source:

Source: *Overseas Trade Statistics of the United Kingdom,* Department of Trade.

*Latin America: Argentina, Bolivia, Brazil, Chile, Colombia, Costa Rica, Cuba, Dominican Republic, Ecuador, El Salvador, Guatemala, Haiti, Honduras, Mexico, Nicaragua, Panama & Canal Zone, Paraguay, Peru, Uruguay and Venezuela.

general. In the first place these can be met by branches putting resolutions to union executives for organisational and financial support for those suffering repression. Such cases very often involve political prisoners and the experience of Chile, Argentina and Uruguay in particular has shown that calls for their release are often effective only if they are backed by the offer of a visa to enter Britain. Since the Conservative government has closed down the Latin American refugee programme the call for its full resumption has become a major issue in addition to demands to stop all arms sales and financial aid to dictatorial regimes. These issues are the fundamental props of solidarity campaigns in Britain.

There are now in Britain broad-based committees for solidarity with Argentina, Brazil, Chile, El Salvador and Nicaragua as well as human rights committees for Central America, Argentina, Bolivia, Chile, Paraguay and Uruguay. In addition to these there is the Joint Working Group for Refugees from Latin America. Aside from collecting up-to-date information and periodically publishing newsletters these organisations very often receive specific requests for assistance and from time to time coordinate visits by Latin American trade unionists looking to build up international solidarity with their struggles. Union affiliation to these organisations strengthens their work immeasurably and provides workers who want to take action with a source of information that can help them be more effective. The addresses of these committees are at the back of the book.

Finally, there is the simple, but often overlooked, fact that solidarity can be a two-way process. Indeed, in the long run it has to be. Clearly British workers are in a privileged position with respect to campaigning for trade union and political freedoms in terms of their stronger economic position. However, collaboration, especially within the same multinational company, can not only broaden support for the demands of workers in another country but also increase knowledge of corporations' international organisation, plans and activities to the benefit of workers both here and elsewhere.

One of the greatest advantages of their international organisation to the large corporations is the ability this gives them to 'divide and rule' their workers throughout the world. Until the workers themselves forge solidarity at that level the opportunities to remove exploitation and transfer wealth to those that create it remain slight.

> **"MARGARET THATCHER IS MOVING IN EXACTLY THE SAME DIRECTION AS WE ARE."**
> Sergio de Castro Spikula, *Chilean Minister of Finance. Quoted in Business News Section.* Sunday Times *6 January 1980.*

PART TWO

Part Two of this book is a brief guide to the trade union movement in Latin America. It is intended as a reference section and consists of a profile of the trade unions in each country of Latin America, and the English-speaking Caribbean countries of Belize, Guyana, Jamaica and Trinidad and Tobago.

The figures for the statistical outlines are taken from the ILO *Year Book of Labour Statistics* (1978 and 1979), the World Bank's *World Development Report* (1978), *Agence Latinoamericaine D'Information* (ALAI) and *Latin American Newsletters* (LANL), unless otherwise mentioned. We have endeavoured to use the most recent and reliable statistics available for each country.

ARGENTINA

POPULATION	26.4 million
ECON. ACTIVE	10.2 million
UNIONISED	36%
UNEMPLOYED	3.9% (Greater Buenos Aires)
LIFE EXPECTANCY	68.2 years

CONFEDERATIONS

Comision de los 25. Independent and technically illegal. The 'group of 25' is one of the successors to the old CGT (Confederacion General de Trabajo), effectively dissolved after the 1976 military coup. The '25' groups unions not formally intervened by the military, represents the more radical peronist tendencies.

CNT — Comision Nacional de Trabajo. Independent but has close relations with the ICFTU. Represents unions intervened by the military and is closer to the government than the '25'. The CNT is larger and more moderate than the '25'.

CUTA — Conduccion Unica de los Trabajadores Argentinos. Established October 1979 but effectively dissolved June 1980 when its component parts — the CNT and the '25' — split over representation on the ILO and ICFTU. The CUTA was nominally illegal but tacitly recognised by the government. Accepted by the ICFTU as representative of the Argentine labour movement.

MAJOR NATIONAL UNIONS

Asociacion Obrera Minera (mineworkers)
Rosario 434-436, Buenos Aires.

Asociacion de Senaleros (signalmen)
Juan B. Justo 763, Buenos Aires.

AOT — Asociacion Obrera Textil (textile workers)
Calle Solis 765, Buenos Aires.

Confederacion Argentina de Trabajadores Estatales (public employees)
Fitzroy 2461, Buenos Aires.

Confederacion de Maestros y Profesores (teachers)
Avenida de Mayo 953, Piso 1, Buenos Aires.

Federacion Argentina de Periodistas (journalists)
Bartolome Mitre 1773, Piso 3, Oficina 305, Buenos Aires.

Federacion de Estibadores Portuarios (dockers)
Estados Unidos 335, Buenos Aires.

Federacion de Obreros y Empleados de la Industria Azucarera (sugar workers)

Federacion de Sindicatos Unidos Petroleros del Estado (oil workers)

Federacion de Trabajadores de Luz y Fuerza (electricity workers)

Federacion Gremial del Personal de la Industria de la Carne (meat workers)

La Fraternidad (footplatemen)
Hipolito Yrigoyen 1938, Buenos Aires.

SMATA — Sindicato de Mecanicos y Afines de Transporte Automotor (car workers)
Bolivar 578, Buenos Aires.

Sindicato de Obreros Maritimos Unidos (seamen)
Necochea 1133, Buenos Aires.

Union Ferroviaria (railway workers)

Union Obrera de Construccion (construction workers)
Rawson 42, Buenos Aires.

UOM — Union Obrera Metalurgica (metal workers) 190,000
Cangallo 1435, Buenos Aires.

Union de Obreros y Empleados Municipales (municipal employees)

Union de Trabajadores de la Industria del Calzado (shoe workers)

The Argentinian labour movement is the oldest and most experienced in Latin America. It is generally considered that the Buenos Aires printers' union was the first proper trade union in the history of the continent. Constituted as a mutalist society in 1857, it won a shorter working day through strike action in 1878. The last two decades of the century witnessed the emergence of other craft unions and the powerful railway workers' union, known as 'La Fraternidad' (1885). The first May Day celebration was in 1890, the year of the creation of the Workers' Federation of the Republic, the first national labour organisation, heavily influenced by anarchosyndicalism. The most bitter strike of this period was the rail strike of 1896 which lasted four months and involved 12,000 workers.

A combination of massive immigration from Europe (over a million people between 1860 and 1900) and rapid economic growth were the chief causes of this social and labour unrest. For the first fifteen years of the twentieth century the leadership of the workers movement was divided between the socialists and the anarcho-syndicalists during a period of expansion and severe repression. In 1905 75 labour organisations attended a congress called by the militant Argentine Workers' Federation (FOA), dominated by the anarcho-syndicalists. The following years saw further splits but unions continued to grow and militancy only eased under the more conciliatory policies of President Saenz Pena who introduced universal suffrage in 1912.

The stimulus to production provided by the First World War combined with the ensuing inflation to cause increased militancy amongst workers. Strikes on the railways, the docks and in the meat packing industry took place in 1917 and 1918. In 1919 a general strike broke out after police had fired on pickets at the British-owned Vasena iron works in Buenos

Aires. Several hundred workers were killed by the army in what became known as the 'Semana Tragica' (Tragic Week). Three years later the rural workers of southern Argentina, who were demanding improvements in their appalling working conditions, met with a similar fate: two thousand died in an onslaught by the army.

Throughout the presidency of Hipolito Yrigoyen (1916-30), who pursued a thoroughly pragmatic policy towards the working class, the labour movement remained weak through its division into competing national confederations, although a semblance of unity was achieved with the founding of the General Confederation of Workers (CGT) in 1930. The other major confederations were the syndicalist USA, the anarchist FORA and the socialist COA. The railway unions, La Fraternidad and the Union Ferroviaria (1922), were the driving force behind the COA (1926). They became something of a labour elite and adopted a reformist position, concentrating on achieving more favourable collective contracts, social security and welfare services for themselves.

The overthrow of Yrigoyen and establishment of a right wing military dictatorship in 1930, combined with internal schisms, held back the development of the labour movement, which was unable to make major advances in the 1930s. In 1935 the anarcho-syndicalists left the CGT which was strengthened the following year by the adherence of the Communist Party-dominated unions but it continued to be under the hegemony of the railway unions which still constituted half the membership in 1942. These inter-war years were a relatively quiet time in the history of the Argentine labour movement.

In 1943 a military coup led by General Ramirez and supported by many junior officers began a process which completely altered the face of Argentine trade unionism. Although the more radical unions were suppressed and the leaders of the main unions ousted, Colonel Juan Peron, the new minister of labour and social welfare, began to court sections of the labour movement which he saw as a potential power base for the new government. Peron's attempt to win the support of the organised working class was made possible by the rapid extension of the economy due to increased income from exports of beef and grain during the war. This expansion worked through to the industrial sector which increased employment, drawing in new labour from the countryside and the periphery of Buenos Aires. Thus, at the same time as thousands of workers without previous political or union attachments entered the industrial workforce, greater revenues facilitated increased state expenditure and the co-optation of important sectors of the urban proletariat.

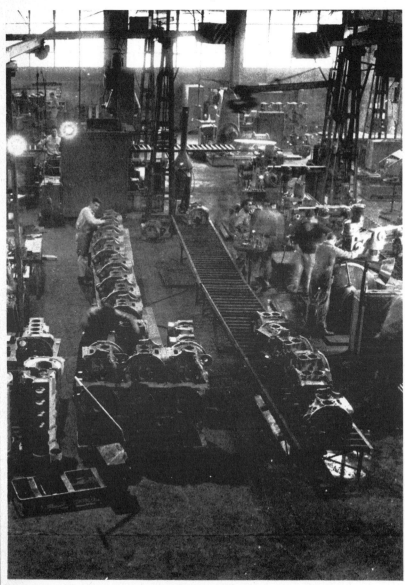

The 1940s witnessed rapid industrialisation in Argentina.

The destroyed headquarters of the Peron's Nationalist Liberation Alliance in Buenos Aires, bombarded in the revolt against him in 1955.

Peron was therefore able to extend favours and important state backing to those unions that were cooperative while at the same time attacking those, predominantly socialist- and communist-backed, which continued to resist state control and influence. The success of this policy was undoubtedly aided by the deep political divisions within the union movement as well as Peron's ability to manipulate state patronage. Between 1943 and 1945 Peron built up considerable personal prestige and when he was finally challenged by the military and dismissed from his post in October 1945, the CGT felt compelled to call a strike which won his release from jail and paved the way for his victory at the polls the following spring.

The welfare laws passed by Peron and the collective industry-wide contracts he fostered significantly increased the standard of living of the working class in the first years of his government. Between 1943 and 1948 real wages rose by 37%. However, Peron's control of the union bureaucracy suffocated the development of any democracy within

the labour movement. The CGT's constitution was changed to proclaim that its fundamental purpose was to support Peron and his policies. All unions that tried to maintain an independent position were refused legal recognition and fourteen major strikes were declared illegal in 1948, with a further 12 outlawed in 1949. In September 1948 5,000 workers at the municipal meat refrigeration plant in Buenos Aires went on strike in protest at the arrest of some of their leaders. The strike was smashed by the police who seriously injured 30 workers. In April 1,000 printing workers were jailed for going on strike. One worker died under torture after the sugar plantation strike of 1949. When the railway unions refused to support Peron's election campaign in 1952, their leaders were forced to resign at gunpoint.

Peron was re-elected as president in 1952 but not in such a euphoric atmosphere as on the previous occasion. Real wages had started falling in 1949 and profit margins were now declining. A combination of military, church and business opposition to Peron led to his overthrow in 1955 but his

prestige was still such that the coup was resisted by the labour movement. Interim President Lonardi did not clamp down on labour organisations completely but his successor, General Aramburu, sought to eradicate peronism from the unions by open repression. The administration of the unions was taken over by government-appointed officials and the CGT was dissolved although it continued to function unofficially. Led by textile workers' leader Andres Framini, it was known as the 'CGT *Negra*' or 'Black CGT'. The peronists of the CGT *Negra* organised opposition to the government and in the two years 1956-57 five million working days were lost through strike action. In 1957 the CGT split into the '62' unions which stayed loyal to Peron, the '32' anti-peronist unions, and the '19' of communist affiliation.

No peronist political party was allowed to contest the 1958 presidential election but Arturo Frondizi made an agreement with Peron in exile whereby he would present himself as a nationalist and anti-imperialist candidate and act in the interests of labour. However, he reneged on his election promises and an angry labour movement staged a general strike in protest. Ten million working days were lost in 1959 alone, and strikes in the meat and oil industries were savagely repressed. The unions were now engaged in a running battle with successive regimes to preserve the advances and social gains they had made under Peron.

In 1962 the peronists were allowed to contest the provincial elections as a legally constituted party but after their overwhelming victory Frondizi was overthrown by a coup. In 1964 three million workers were involved in the occupation of 11,000 factories. They demanded the release of political and trade union prisoners, the abolition of repressive legislation, the legalisation of those unions banned by the government, full employment, worker participation in the management of companies, strict control of the prices of basic necessities, protection for national industry, the end of the state of siege, a return to the constitution, agrarian reform and an end to the political ban on the peronist party.

Meanwhile the government did end direct control of the CGT which, in 1963, held its first ordinary congress since the fall of Peron. The conflict between the two wings of the movement sharpened, ending in the victory of Augusto Vandor of the UOM who, as general secretary of the CGT, reached an agreement with a sector of the military to support the coup in 1966 against President Illia in return for CGT participation in the new government. However, the new president, General Ongania, banned strikes, froze wages, and placed the leading unions under government control.

The hardline peronists had stayed in the CGT despite Vandor's control of the organisation but when they were deprived of their victory at the 1968 union elections the CGT split again, with Raimundo Ongaro establishing an opposition CGT known as the CGT of the Argentines (CGTA) or the CGT Paseo Colon. The leadership of Vandor's 'participationist' sector refused to oppose the military regime while Ongaro's wing faced persecution by organising industrial action in defence of workers' living standards and trade union rights.

A landmark in the history of the Argentinian trade union movement came in May 1969 with the 'Cordobazo'. The killing of two students by police sparked a massive wave of protest that swept the industrial centres of the country. The struggle was fiercest in Cordoba where parts of the city were occupied by car workers and students in an unprecedented display of mass opposition to the regime. Many people were killed and the government were badly shaken. The 'Cordobazo' was the culmination of a decade of worker dissatisfaction and was an important step in the succession of events that were to bring Peron back to power, nearly 20 years after he had been overthrown. After the fall of Ongania, mainly as a result of the 'Cordobazo', General Lanusse (1971-73) was obliged to permit limited political activity and eventually union and political pressure forced the government to call elections. The peronist candidate, Hector Campora, was elected and paved the way for the return of Peron from exile in Spain in 1973.

However, Peron was now much more conservative and acting in totally different political and economic circumstances to those of the 1940s. The division in the peronist movement deepened as the 'loyalists' of the union bureaucracies attacked workers who engaged in strike action against the wage freeze imposed by the government or who joined the opposition to the 'old guard'. It was in this period that a new type of rank and file organisation, the 'coordinadora', emerged as an alternative leadership to the collaborationist bureaucrats. The number of strikes increased and it became plain that while the majority of the working class still remained sentimentally attached to Peron many were able to see the flagrant contradiction between the movement's rhetoric and its practice.

It was Peron's own minister of social welfare, Jose Lopez Rega, who organised the infamous 'Triple A' death squad which assassinated union and political militants, thus setting a pattern for the security forces of General Videla and drawing retaliation from the militants, escalating the level of violence in the workers movement. Industrial turmoil increased with striking workers responding to the government's austerity plans by demanding wage rises, basic reforms and an end to repression. In 1974 Peron died and was succeeded as president by his wife, Isabela. Isabela retained the support of CGT leaders, including the powerful head of the UOM, Lorenzo Miguel, but her economic policies were rejected by the mass of workers. In March 1975 leaders opposed to the general secretary of the UOM were elected to office in the key steel producing area of Villa Constitucion. The regime's response was to send in the security forces who arrested almost all the oppositionists. (Some of these leaders, such as Alberto Piccinini, Juan Acuna and Benicio Bernachea, are still in prison and have been adopted as political prisoners by groups in Britain).

In July 1975 a spate of wildcat stoppages forced the CGT into declaring a 48-hour general strike which paralysed the country and obliged the government to dismiss Lopez Rega. But in March 1976 the military staged their long awaited coup which unleashed massive and systematic repression of the labour movement on the pattern established by the military dictatorships in Chile and Uruguay three years earlier.

The military junta led by General Videla banned trade union activity and appointed military officers to take charge of the CGT and all important unions. The military had used the months before the coup to prepare lists of union militants and many hundreds of these were immediately arrested.

General Videla

Amnesty International has estimated that as many as 15,000 people have been kidnapped by the armed forces since the coup, and shop floor militants have been among the chief targets. Physical repression has been accompanied by an economic policy that has slashed the real wages of working people. Martinez de Hoz, the economy minister, is hated as much as Videla himself. Massive cuts in public spending, the free play of market forces, maximisation of profits through the enforced decline in labour costs and the elimination of all political opposition are all central policies of the regime but the adoption of monetarist policies has not been as wholehearted as in Chile and Uruguay, at least in part because the Argentine government has placed importance on retaining the traditionally high level of employment.

Despite physical intimidation the labour movement has resisted this unprecedented attact on its rights and economic position. Strikes have taken place in several sectors since the coup: motor industry and power workers in 1976; rail, oil, bank and maritime workers in 1977; dockers and railway workers in 1978. The repression and high inflation (175% in 1978) provoked a general strike in April 1979 in which 30% of workers participated — under the circumstances a clear demonstration of popular opposition to the regime. Although the National Commission of Labour (CNT), which groups those unions 'intervened' by the military, did not participate in the strike it later agreed to form a central national labour body with the *Comison de los 25* to negotiate with the regime on labour matters. This body, formed in October 1979, is known as the Conduccion Unica de Trabajadores Argentinos (CUTA), and was tacitly accepted by the regime. However, most union activity continued to be organised locally and in the utmost secrecy outside of the formal structures, partly because of fear of repression, partly because the large organisations have either entered into discreet and partial negotiations with the regime or have proved unable to coordinate action.

Under the government's long-awaited *Ley de Asociaciones Profesionales* or Labour Code, published in November 1979, national labour confederations and the CGT have been abolished, unions are banned from all political activity, the closed shop is outlawed and the social welfare provided by the unions is to be taken over by the state. The failure of the union leaderships to achieve unity through CUTA may be seen as yet another round of bureaucratic wrangling that has dogged the unions in recent decades but it is clear that with the labour movement under such vehement attack the effects are likely to be severe and may well prejudice resistance to the labour code when the combativity of the working class is growing but its organisation still remains very weak.

IKA-Renault workers march on the centre of Cordoba. It is the beginning of the *'Cordabazo'* workers' revolt—1969.

BELIZE

POPULATION	140,000 (estimate)
ECON. ACTIVE	30,000 (estimate)
UNIONISED	22% (estimate)
UNEMPLOYED	
LIFE EXPECTANCY	

CONFEDERATIONS

NFW — National Federation of Workers. Affil. CLAT.

TUC — Trades Union Congress Affil. ORIT.

UNIONS

NTU – National Teachers Union 200

POU – Public Officers Union 500

UGWU – United General Workers Unions (March 1979) 3,000

During the first half of this century, extremely harsh labour laws held back the growth of labour oganisations in Belize, then known as British Honduras, one of the two British colonies in Latin America. Labour unrest in the 1930s led the British to pass the Trade Union Ordinance (1941) which legalised trade union activity. However, a further ordinance, which was not repealed until 1953, forbade strikes in the timber industry. In general, labour organisations were severely hampered by colonial restrictions on their activity.

The first union to be registered in Belize was the British Honduras Trade Union (1943). This name was soon changed to the General Workers Union (GWU). It was founded by a group of shipwrights in the capital, Belize City, and quickly spread to the rest of the country. In 1950, the leaders of the young trade union movement formed the country's first political party, the Peoples' United Party (PUP) and laid the foundations for the Belizean nationalist movement.

Prolonged strikes against the Belize Estate and Produce Company, the main timber concern and the country's largest employer, and against the Colonial Development Corporation and Public Works Department coupled with internal diversions almost destroyed the GWU, but the 1960s saw a revival in the fortunes of the labour movement. The amalgamation in 1979 of the GWU, strong in the capital, and the Southern Christian Union, strong in the citrus and rice growing south, marked an important advance for the labour movement. Led by the radicals Stephen Latchman and Misheck Mawema, the United General Workers Union (UGWU) supports the moderate left-wing government of George Price and the PUP, re-elected in the 1979 general elections on its policies of independence from Britain and rejection of all Guatemalan territorial claims to Belize.

BOLIVIA

POPULATION	4.6 million
ECON. ACTIVE	1.5 million
UNIONISED	
UNEMPLOYED	4.5%
LIFE EXPECTANCY	48.2 years

CONFEDERATION

COB — Central Obrera Boliviana (1952). No international affiliation. Includes all important unions and other popular organisations such as housewives' and tenants' associations. Apartado 1379, La Paz.

MAJOR UNIONS

Confederacion de Ferroviarios, Ramas y Anexas (railway workers) Yanacocha 68, La Paz.

CONSTBRA — Confederation de Sindicatos de Trabajadores Bancarios (bank workers)

Confederacion de Trajadores en Construccion (construction workers) Boqueron 1234, La Paz.

Confederacion de Transportistas y Choferes (transport workers)

CGTFB — Confederacion General de Trabajadores Fabriles (factory workers)

Confederacion Nacional de Maestros Urbanos y Rurales (teachers)

CSUTC — Confederacion Sindical Unica de Trabajadores Campesinos (peasants)

CUB — Confederacion Universitaria Boliviana (students)

FSTMB — Federacion de Sindicatos de Trabajadores Mineros de Bolivia (1944) Apartado 1379, La Paz.

Bolivia has one of the most militant, best organised and politically conscious labour movements in Latin America. The miners have always been in the vanguard of the struggle for trade union rights and social justice and it is their union, the FSTMB, which dominates the history of the labour movement.

The second half of the nineteenth century witnessed the creation of many mutualist societies but it was not until the establishment of the printworkers' union in 1905 that the first Bolivian trade union was born. In the following year May Day was celebrated for the first time and a group of artisans organised the Workers' Social Centre. The workers gradually improved their organisation and in 1919 the League of Railway Workers and Employees, which played a leading role in the post-war period, was formed. In 1921 the railway workers went on strike and 10,000 workers demonstrated in La Paz against restrictions on the labour movement and the increase in the length of the working day. It was the Railway Workers' Federation that called the first national workers congress in 1921.

Although President Bautista Saavedra took power in 1920 with promises of social reform, the contraction in the world economy and the consequent decrease in the price of tin led to restrictions on the right to unionise and harsh repression of the miners. When the Central Workers' Federation of Uncia was founded in 1923 a series of conflicts led to a massacre of workers, women and children in the camp. Despite the nominal establishment of an eight hour working day in 1926 the workers made little progress in this period in terms of both working conditions and their own organisation. A major turning point came with the Chaco War (1932-35), in which Bolivia fought Paraguay for possession of the Chaco desert and the oil that was believed to be under it. Bolivia's defeat in the war discredited the government and increased the political consciousness of many soldiers and workers. Between 1936 and 1939 Colonels Toro and Busch enacted legislation favourable to workers and unions began to organise more freely. A ministry of labour and the Union Confederation of Bolivian Workers were established. However, these governments failed to make any impact on the economic and social structure of the country and in 1939 the tin oligarchy was able to regain control after this period of political confusion. When, in 1942, the miners refused to accept the government's rejection of their wage demands, the army massacred 400 workers at the Catavi camp. The increase in repression encouraged the emergence of the populist Nationalist Revolutionary Movement (MNR) which supported the coup of leftist junior officers led by Colonel Villaroel in 1943. The Union Federation of Bolivian Mine Workers (FSTMB) was established under the more favourable political conditions provided by this regime, which itself proceeded to sponsor the first national peasants' congress in recognition of the extemely backward conditions and lack of organisation of the rural workers who were by the far and largest sector of the population.

All the social gains made by the labour movement were wiped out when Villarroel was overthrown by a bloody right wing uprising in 1946. The following year witnessed the so-called 'Masacra blanca' (white massacre) of Catavi when all the miners were sacked and then re-contracted minus the militants. A Committee of Workers' Coordination was set up but the regime froze all union back accounts, blacklisted militants, harassed union leaders and imposed the mine owners' plans for the reorganisation of the industry. But the resilient miners' union was not broken, and in 1949 the regime sought a violent confrontation in order to destroy their organisation for good. Union leaders were arrested all over the country. The miners replied by seizing North America and Scandanavian engineers as hostages and answered the army's rifles with the dynamite they used every day in their work. At the same time the MNR, which had effectively gone underground since the fall of Villarroel, launched a revolt that led to a month-long civil war. However, with US backing the army proved able to maintain control and the miners once again had to reorganise clandestinely.

A new period in the history of the Bolivian labour movement opened in 1952 when the workers, led by the MNR, overthrew a military junta after three days of fighting. The newly formed Bolivian Labour Centre (COB), which was largely the creation of the FSTMB, emerged as the centre of power and became the focus of workers' control, and the expropriation of large estates, as outlined in the miners' Thesis of Pulacayo which had been drawn up in 1946 under the influence of the Trotskyist Workers' Revolu-

An underground tin worker has a life expectancy of 35 years.

Once he dies or has to retire due to ill health the mining company will evict his family from their home.

Miners no longer fit to work underground try to scrape a living from reworking the slag.

tionary Party (POR). The MNR government, which contained members of the COB, was obliged to nationalise the mines, institute universal suffrage and initiate an agrarian reform. The National Confederation of Bolivian Peasants was established and Juan Lechin, the miners' leader, was minister of labour and mines for a short time. However, the MNR moved increasingly rightwards and sought to gain political control of the COB at the latter's 1954 congress. The cornerstone of President Hernan Siles Suazo's (1956-60) economic policy was the stabilisation plan imposed by the International Monetary Fund (IMF). Unemployment, inflation and declining production hit workers' living standards severely as the government froze wages. In 1958 the FSTMB congress was violently broken up by government supporters. The conservative policies of the 'revolutionary' government, which still enjoyed a degree of prestige as a result of the MNR's leading role in the 1952 Revolution, deepened the division and demoralisation of the working class, including the miners.

In 1964 General Rene Barrientos took power in a right wing military coup. Although he talked of the 'irreversible reforms' of 1952, Barrientos brutally repressed a national miners' strike in 1965 when Lechin and some 60 other union leaders were exiled, local unions dismantled and the mining areas occupied by the army. Many workers were killed and around 5,000 were sacked in another *masacra blanca*. The same sequence of events occurred in 1967 when the military moved to forestall the holding of a secret workers' congress in the mines. On the night of San Juan at least 20 people were killed as soldiers invaded and took over the mining villages.

Barrientos was of peasant stock and spoke the main peasant language, Quechua, fluently. This enabled him to forge an alliance between the army and the peasants, known as the Military-Peasant Pact. The miners were caricatured by Barrientos as dynamite-wielding madmen bent on making personal gain out of the country's most precious resource. The success of the Pact divided the two principal sections of the labour movement and it was not until 1979 that large sections of the peasantry broke from this alliance and sided with the industrial working class.

After the death of Barrientos in 1969 General Ovando took power and, under considerable pressure from the workers, nationalised the US multinational Gulf Oil. However, this was too much for the army and Ovando was overthrown after a year when a military triumvirate took power in October 1970. The generals' coup was met by a general strike in which the reorganised and much recovered unions put their weight behind the populist General Juan Jose Torres who reversed the coup and took

Siglo XX union headquarters, frequently the target of army attacks.

power. The state security law was repealed and the FSTMB and the COB both held congresses. A Popular Assembly, organised by the COB and the major parties of the left, emerged as the organ of popular power and entered into conflict with Torres over the course of the 'revolution'. Delegates to the Assembly were elected from the shop floor and regional assemblies were also set up in an unprecedented experiment of democratic working class political mobilisation. But the coup led by Colonel Hugo Banzer in August 1971 cut short the development of this challenge and in a bloody offensive forced the labour movement into headlong retreat. The Assembly was dissolved, left wing parties banned, unions driven into clandestinity and many students and workers killed. A massive devaluation of the peso led to a huge increase in the earnings of exporters and a severe decline in the living standards of the poorest sectors of the population.

The Banzer regime's systematic violation of human rights and its brutal repression of all opposition brought international condemnation and national resistance. After a miners' strike in 1974 the government placed a complete ban on all forms of production stoppage and replaced all union officials with pro-government labour co-ordinators. But the miners maintained their independent organisation underground and in 1976 once again went on strike demanding a wage increase, the end of the military occupation of the mining zones and an amnesty for the exiled and imprisoned union leaders. It was only after six weeks and by siege tactics that the army broke the strike. Twenty five union leaders and militants were exiled to Chile to be dealt with by the Pinochet dictatorship. It was in the following year, 1977, that a delegation from the NUM secretly visited Bolivia and Chile, and put pressure on the British government to withdraw financial aid to the state mining corporation COMIBOL, as requested by the FSTMB.

Under growing domestic and international pressure Banzer announced elections for 1978. A hunger strike started by relatives of political prisoners and exiles in January 1978 was supported by hundreds of people across the country with the call for an unrestricted amnesty and full union and political freedoms. Banzer's position weakened and he was forced to concede the amnesty and allow unions to operate openly. In May 1978 the FSTMB held its congress without hindrance and elected Lechin once again as executive secretary. This was a year of reorganisation and workers sought to restore their wages to the levels prior to the 1971 coup.

The result of the 1978 elections was annulled after ballot rigging had failed to prevent the victory of the centre-left UDP coalition led by MNR veteran Hernan Siles Suazo. General Juan Pereda, Banzer's candidate, took power in a coup but was rapidly displaced by a group of young officers led by General David Padilla and favourable to the restoration of parliamentary democracy. The new government decreed a 70% increase in wages for the miners and ordered the private companies to implement it. New elections were held in June 1979 but these produced no decisive result and power was handed over to the president of congress, Walter Guevara who, like Padilla, tried to steer a middle course while preparations were made for yet another poll.

This process was brought to an abrupt end in November 1979 when, after a period of escalating tension, the reactionary Colonel Albert Natusch staged a coup. The COB immediately called a general strike and within a day the country was paralysed. Natusch's troops engaged with students and workers in the streets and several hundred people were killed in two weeks of intermittent fighting. The workers stood firm and it was the miners, who steadfastly refused to return to work even

Bolivian workers resist the tanks of Colonel Natusch in November '79; the Colonel's coup fails, but over 300 people die in the struggle against him.

after the COB had called off the general strike, that led the opposition to Natusch who left the country after 16 days. Power was restored to congress and the president of the house of deputies, Lidia Gueiler, became president. However, Natusch's allies remained in control of the armed forces and by the end of 1979 it was apparent that the

FSTMB union headquarters ransacked and bombed during the November '79 coup attempt.

civilian regime was powerless to act against them. The first months of 1980 saw a strengthening of this right wing faction and the growing threat of a coup to reverse the 'democratic experiment' for good. This possibility was increased with the deepening of the economic crisis in Bolivia and further class polarisation. However, these months also evidenced great advances in the organisation of the working class and particularly of the peasantry which, for the first time, consolidated an independent union structure in alliance with the COB. In the climate of growing political tension and antagonism this alliance stands to be tested very harshly before long.*

* On July 17 1980, as this book was going to press, a right wing military coup led by General Luis Garcia Meza forestalled the inauguration of a new constitutional government following elections in June. In the first days of this new dictatorship worker and peasant resistance has been strong, with the army encountering steadfast opposition to its attempts to occupy the mining camps. Several union leaders, including Simon Reyes of the FSTMB, have been assassinated and Juan Lechin, amongst others, kidnapped by the armed forces.

BRAZIL

POPULATION	116.8 million
ECON. ACTIVE	39.7 million
UNIONISED	
UNEMPLOYED	26% (including underemployment)
LIFE EXPECTANCY	63.4 years

CONFEDERATIONS

CNTI — Confederacao Nacional de Trabalhadores da Industria (1947). Largest confederation with 55 federations and 1240 local unions. Affil. ORIT until 1971. Several affiliates have links with the International Metalworkers Federation.

CNTC — Confederacao Nacional de Trabalhadores da Comercial (1947). Affil. ORIT. Membership drawn from a variety of occupations including workers in the coffee trade.

CONTAG — Confederaco Nacional de Trabalhadores da Agricultura (1973). Independent. 2275 branches with five million workers (1979).

CUT — Central Unica de Trabalhadores. (Formation announced 22/6/79, but still not put into effect).

Other Confederations include: CNTTT (Land Transport Workers), CNTTMFA (Maritime, River and Air Transport Workers), CONTCOP (Communications and Publicity Workers), CONTEC (Insurance and Bank Workers), CONTEEC (Education and Cultural Workers).

In May 1978, a wave of strikes swept through the city of Sao Paulo, marking the return of the labour movement to the centre of the stage in Brazilian politics. Workers have forcefully asserted their claims, gained in self-confidence, and improved their organisation. This new militancy is aimed at improving living standards kept low by a govern-ment determined to keep labour costs down to a minimum. Secondly, it represents an attack on the state trade union system introduced by President Vargas in the late 1930s, and refined by the regime which came to power with the military coup of 1964. The strikes of 1978 and 1979 have forced pay increases, but employers have responded by sacking union militants, and the wages policy introduced by the government in November 1979, is intended to concede minor points while maintaining the old system intact. Despite the recent liberal-isation measures, Brazil's poli-tical future is still in the balance and there is a very real danger that the government will revert to its previous strong arm tactics if it feels that the independent action of the unions is threatening its control.

The first major strikes in the history of the Brazilian labour movement took place in the early years of this century as the rate of economic develop-ment in the coastal cities began to increase. These were met by police repression, the imprison-ment and deportation of leaders, and rigorous anti-labour legis-lation. A product of these struggles was the Labour Confederation of Brazil (COB), formed in 1906. That same year strikes paralysed many sectors of the economy, and won some concessions from employers. But a combination of government repression and weak organis-ation meant that workers failed to make significant progress in their fight for better working conditions and basic trade union rights. Rail, textile, and port workers were prominent in this early period which witnessed a major strike against the British-owned Great Western Railway in 1909, a general strike which paralysed Sao Paulo for several

In-plant march by steelworkers supporting the wage demands of the Sao Paulo metal-workers, October 1978. Em Tempo

days in 1917 and a series of strikes in the major cities in the period 1917-19. The 1920s was a difficult time for labour with the so-called 'Infamous Law' or *'Lei Infame'* applying stiff penalties to those participating in workers organisations and a state of siege was in force between the years 1922 and 1926. In 1929 the General Confederation of Workers was formed under the influence of the Communist Party.

The autonomous development of the labour movement was interrupted during the 1930s when the government of Getulio Vargas took control of its destiny. In 1930, Vargas overthrew the landowning oligarchy that had ruled the country since the old Portuguese emperor was deposed in 1891. The Colour Law of 1931 granted legal recognition to trade unions for the first time and a series of decrees the following year established the eight hour working day, arbitration procedures for labour disputes, and a measure of job security. However, in 1937, Vargas wiped the slate clean and imposed the so-called *'Estado Novo'* (New State) modelled on Mussolini's Italian corporate state. Since then there have been no properly independent legal unions in Brazil.

The *estado novo* with its emphasis on the 'national interest' and its denial of the class struggle, strove to neutralise social conflict at a time of rapid economic development and regulate the labour market during the process of industrialisation. It instituted a series of measures favourable to the working class such as social security, pensions, paid holidays and minimum wage legislation, and it confirmed the labour legislation of 1931-32. However, legal recognition was withdrawn from all existing unions and a rigidly hierarchical system of local unions, regional federations and national confederations responsible to the minister of labour was instituted on a sectoral basis. All workers automatically paid one day's wage every year to maintain this administrative structure and finance the government's social welfare programme. The money raised in this way is currently distributed by the Central Bank in the following proportions: local unions — 60%, federations — 15%, confederations — 5%, and ministry of labour — 20%.

Neither strikes nor direct collective bargaining were permitted, and a system of labour courts regulated all differences between workers and employers. The unions became little more than docile agencies for the administration of the government's social welfare programme. No central unifying independent labour organisation was allowed to exist. These laws, codified in the Consolidated Labour Law (CLT) of 1943 were to remain in force long after the demise of the *estado novo*. To this day, the labour movement is struggling to free itself from the restrictions and controls imposed by this system.

Vargas, who had begun to adopt an openly pro-labour stance, was forced out of office in 1945. After initial hesitation, the newly elected President Dutra clamped down on the wave of trade union activity that accompanied Vargas' fall and retained the labour legislation of the 1930s. The return of Vargas to the presidency in 1950, this time by popular election, marked the beginning of a long period in which the labour movement made significant advances. Although the *estado novo* laws remained in force, control over the trade unions was relaxed and a liberal political atmosphere prevailed throughout the 1950s. The emphasis was on economic expansion, particularly under President Kubitscheck (1956-60), who called for '50 years development in five years'. The most dramatic advance in the organisation of workers took place in the north-east of the country where hundreds of peasant leagues were formed between 1955 and 1964.

Labour found a champion in Vargas' minister of labour, Joao Goulart, who went on to become vice-president and then President of the Republic (1961-64). In the early 1960s, trade union leaders had enormous political influence, but although a General Labour Command (CGT) was formed in 1962, the labour movement failed to develop an effective and autonomous organisational structure. During a severe economic and political crisis, the military intervened, dissolved congress, outlawed existing political parties, and purged the trade unions. This was a severe lesson for the labour movement which had its power through the influence it had over a radical but indecisive populist politician who was unable to tackle the basic social and economic problems of the country.

The military coup of May 1964 prefigured the events of a decade later in Chile and Argentina. Though less violent and less dramatic than the coups in the latter two countries, it was just as successful in silencing all opposition to the regime. The new military government already had to hand a body of legislation and a trade union structure which enabled tight control over the labour movement. A mixture of physical repression, the takeover of 400 unions, and modifications to the labour law, such as a draconian anti-strike law, the suspension of wage bargaining (1964), and the abolition of job security provisions (1966), effectively stifled resistance to the government's harsh economic policies.

Annual wage increases were

fixed by a complicated mathematical equation formulated by the government and designed to achieve a decline in labour costs. It has been calculated that the real value of industrial wages fell by 15% between 1964 and 1975, the period of the great Brazilian 'economic miracle'. It remains a common tactic for employers to sack workers just before the annual wage review and then re-employ them at the old rates. An indication of the pauperisation of the working class was given by the deterioration of health standards. Even the authorities were alarmed when a meningitis epidemic in 1974 claimed the lives of 3,000 people in Sao Paulo alone. To maintain its grip on the labour movement and prevent the emergence of any radical leadership, the government ensured that its own men, popularly known as '*pelegos*', were voted into all key union posts.

The labour movement's answer to this pressure was to organise action on the shop floor independent of the formal union structure. In April and July 1968, major wildcat strikes by metalworkers and student demonstrations were crushed by the army. Sweeping arrests were made and trade unionists died under torture. The wave of repression reduced the labour movement to its lowest point. In the early 1970s, workers felt their way more carefully in their attempts to put pressure on employers. Typical of the many bulletins secretly distributed at the time was the 'Manifesto of the Sao Paulo Metalworkers Trade Union Opposition' of 1974. 'A great deal is said about the Brazilian miracle', it said, 'but for us the miracle is how we manage to survive on the low wages we receive. Because of this, we have to work 12 or 13 hours a day and many of us work on Sundays. In practice, this signifies the

Prisoners taken during 1968 strike in Osasco.

elimination of one of the working class's greatest conquests: the eight hour day and a weekly rest day'. To combat the sustained attack on their living standards, workers formed ad hoc shop floor committees, the so-called 'factory commissions'. Such tactics as go-slows, work to rule and overtime bans won small pay increases from the transnational companies, particularly in the automobile industry.

During the presidencies of Generals Geisel (1974-79) and Figueiredo (1979-), the government, under increasing pressure from many sectors of society, yet confident of its ability to control political developments, has eased repression and introduced a series of reforms. Despite negative economic trends caused by the energy crisis and the burden of a huge

"*It's more practical to divide the profit among 2000 Generals than among 100 million Brazilians*" Ruis, Siempre, Mexico City

foreign debt, the government has been unwilling to compromise these reforms by acting forcefully against a resurgent labour movement. There is also support in business circles for a rise in the standard of living of the working class at a time when the stagnation of the world economy and growing protectionism in the industrialised countries are making the further development of the home market a more attractive proposition. There was also widespread concern about the possibility of serious unrest if concessions were not granted to workers in the immediate future.

The chain of events leading to the recent massive strikes can be traced back to the summer of 1977 when it was revealed that the government statistics used to calculate the annual wage increases for 1973 had been falsified to the detriment of workers. Labour demands for the payment of arrears led to an unprecedented meeting between union leaders and government ministers, but this failed to produce any results. However, as workers sensed a change in the political atmosphere, they began to express their opinions more boldly. For example, a manifesto signed by 110 trade unions from the state of Rio Grande do Sul protested at the government's economic policies and demanded the right of workers to negotiate wages directly with employers.

Then, in May 1978, metal, engineering and textile workers in the industrial belt around Sao Paulo went on strike. Workers arrived at the factories but refused to turn on the machines. The government was unsure exactly how to deal with the protest and agreement over a wage increase was soon reached, but the strike undermined the government's position and encouraged other sectors of the labour movement to defend their rights. A teachers' strike in Sao Paulo closed 1,850 schools, and gained widespread popular support. Oil, bank, and port workers all took industrial action. This wave of strikes resulted in only limited material gains but increased self-confidence.

The Sao Paulo engineering workers congress of September outlined the main objectives of the labour movement, although the subsequent industrial action demonstrated some of its weaknesses. With the workers in a militant mood, the new generation of independent leaders triumphed over the *pelegos*. A six-point programme was adopted calling for collective bargaining to be the basic procedure in all disputes, the establishment of workers' commissions at a shop floor level, the definitive recognition of the right to strike, and the establishment of a central labour organisation. The engineers went straight into action to back up their demands: in October, 240,000 workers went on strike in support of a 70% pay claim and the right to set up workers' commissions. A coordinated response from employers and procedural tricks by *pelego* leaders such as Joaquim dos Santos Andrade, nicknamed 'Judas' by the workers, combined to confuse and isolate workers. Many strike organisers were sacked and blacklisted, and the only gain was a moderate wage rise.

Workers continued to press their claims in 1979 with varying degrees of success. In March, a strike by 180,000 metalworkers in Sao Paulo marked a further advance in the development of working class militancy and organisation. The main demands of the strike were a 77% wage rise and official management recognition of shop floor union delegates. General Figueriedo's first act as President was to decree the strike illegal and suspend the leader of the metalworkers, Luis Ignacio da Silva, popularly known as 'Lula', from his union post. However, the government was anxious for industrial peace and employers were concerned at the huge financial losses caused by the dispute. A compromise was reached with agreement on a wage rise and the re-instatement of Lula. The further experience gained from the strike compensated for the fact that the issue of union delegates remained outstanding. Lula has now emerged as a major trade union leader.

The bus drivers of Rio de Janeiro, the construction workers of Belo Horizonte and the sugar plantation workers of the north-east made significant gains in late 1979 after taking industrial action. There have been rumblings of discontent in the army about the 'tolerance' being displayed by the government. Delfim Neto, the planning minister, recently said that 'if we want a society that is politically open, we have to understand that strikers are a part of it'. However, the government reacted harshly against striking engineering workers in Sao Paulo, Guaralhos and Osasco in November 1979. The arrest of 700 union activists and the shooting by police of a strike leader on picket duty indicated that the repressive apparatus was still very much intact.

The increasing militancy evident in the strike movements of 1978 and 1979 was not, however, dimmed by the coercive action of the state. Between March 31 and May 11 1980 nearly 350,000 car workers staged the most important strike in the country since 1968, crippled the car industry for six weeks, and issued a forthright challenge to the transnationals and the military regime. The principal plants affected were the Sao Paulo factories of Chrysler, Ford,

Mercedes Benz and Volkswagen. Although radical by the standards of Brazil, the workers' demands were extraordinarily moderate compared to those of workers employed by these firms in other countries. Of the 30 concrete demands put to the employers the most central were those of job security for one year (a particularly sensitive issue after the lay-offs following the previous years' strikes); a 15% wage rise plus a cost of living increase; wages to be indexed to a three-month inflation rate; a stop to job rotation which impedes wage increases for seniority; access to the shopfloor for union leaders; freedom to put up union notices without censorship; and a 40 hour week.

When the regional labour court ruled the strike illegal a further 325,000 workers from 38 municipalities in Sao Paulo joined the stoppage and the car industry was so severely hit that Volkswagen went so far as to offer a full day's pay to anyone who would work for an hour and a guarantee of five years' employment to all toolmakers who returned to work immediately. But 90% of the workforce stayed out. On April 17 the government replaced the democratically elected union leaders of Sao Bernardo and Santo Andre with *pelegos*, and two days later arrested Lula along with 33 other union leaders. Meetings were broken up with force and workers in the post of Santos, where solidarity action was being undertaken, were jailed. The Church came out in open support of the workers' claims, arranged supplies of food for the strikers' families and provided space for meetings when the police ousted workers from public property.

Deprived of their leadership, the strikers continued for another two weeks but by May 11 they began to go back, defeated by hunger rather than loss of spirit. On the surface the strike appeared to have ended in disaster: nearly 1,000 workers fired without severance pay, a rise of only 7% with no job guarantees, no shorter hours, and the loss of the authentic union leadership. However, the sheer duration of the strike, its extent and massive popular support shook the regime very badly, dispelled any illusions in its self-proclaimed policy of 'abertura', resulted in losses of over £1,000 million for the transnationals, and served to underline the importance of political organisation for the working class. With the formation of Lula's Workers' Party (PT) it is likely that the painful and erratic resurgence of the union movement in Brazil will gain a political voice it has lacked for so long. The setbacks suffered in the spring of 1980 were grave but they point to renewed struggle.

Women workers in Volkswagen's Sao Paulo plant, Brazil. USPG

CHILE

POPULATION	10.3 million
ECON. ACTIVE	3.3 million
UNIONISED	
UNEMPLOYED	13.5% (National Statistical Institute of Chile)
LIFE EXPECTANCY	64.4 years

CONFEDERATIONS

CNS — Coordinadora Nacional Sindical (1978, banned Oct. 1978). Includes construction, textile, engineering and mine workers as well as peasant federations.

FUT — Frente Unitario de Trabajadores. Affil. CLAT.

Group of Ten or Consejo Nacional de Organizaciones Sindicales Democraticos (1976). Affil. ORIT.

Trade Union Defence Command (August 1979) groups all the above, which may be contacted through the Vicaria Pastoral Obrera, Santa Monica 2360, Santiago.

UNTRACH — Union Nacional de Trabajadores Chilenos. Government body.

The Chilean labour movement is one of the oldest in the continent. The last decades of the nineteenth century witnessed continuous social and labour unrest. In 1890, a wave of strikes swept through the country and 50 people were killed in Valparaiso when women attacked stores in protest at the high cost of living. In this early period, workers were organised in mutualist societies, resistance societies, and unions known as 'mancomunales'. The mancomunales were the typical form of union organisation in the northern nitrate fields which were as important to the Chilean economy as copper is now. Repression reached a peak in the first decade of this century with a series of massacres of maritime workers, railwaymen and, most infamous of all, nitrate workers at Iquique in 1907, when 2,000 people were killed by the army.

The first national workers' organisation, the Labour Federation of Chile (FOCH) was formed in 1909 largely as a response to the repression of the labour movement. In the following years, the FOCH organised workers in pursuit of such basic demands as the eight hour working day and minimum wage legislation.

After the Russian Revolution, the confederation took a more militant stance and joined the Red International of trade unions (1921). It called for workers' control of industrial production and the abolition of capitalism. Meanwhile, anarchist unions established the Regional Labour Federation (FOR) in 1919, but this organisation never approached the influence of the FOCH.

In 1920, Allesandri was the first Chilean president to be elected with the open support of sectors of the working class. Hopes for social advance were soon dashed however, and the nitrate miners again suffered a massacre at the hands of the army. Social security and labour legislation was introduced in 1924, but the government's attitude to the labour movement can be gauged by the tone of the new labour code which stated: 'the unions established in conformity with the provisions of the code will be institutions of mutual collaboration between the factors of production, and therefore those organisations which impede discipline and order in work will be considered contrary to the spirit and norm of the law'.

The following years saw an increase in repression under the dictatorship of Ibanez (1927-31) who tried to replace existing organisations with a state-sponsored union confederation. Repression combined with unemployment to demoralise workers and cause a decline in the labour movement. Following the fleeting 'socialist republic' of 1932 workers were again put on the defensive with hundreds killed or deported after army intervention in strikes. The FOCH was persecuted and lost all influence.

Its place was taken by the Confederation of Chilean Workers (CTC) formed in 1936 as a part of the movement towards unity among the left that was to result in the Popular Front government of Cerda (1938-41). The CTC mobilised popular support for the government and led the campaign to unionise Chilean workers. Between 1938 and 1941, the number of trade union members rose by 50,000. A further 50,000 were added in the following three years. However, CTC unity collapsed in the 1940s when the Socialist and Communist Parties broke their alliance. In 1948, the Law in Defence of Democracy drove the communists underground and placed severe restrictions on the labour movement.

Workers fought back, and in 1950, white collar unions led a general strike which had widespread support. The government was forced to abandon a wage freeze and grant an amnesty to union leaders arrested in previous strikes. The early 1950s saw another move towards unity in the labour movement, and in

1952, a National Commission for Trade Union Unity called for measures such as increases in wages linked to the cost of living; the repeal of the Law in Defence of Democracy; control of basic sectors of the economy; the participation of workers in the running and development of industry; a workers' housing plan; agrarian reform; an end to the military pact with the United States; the establishment of relations with all countries of the world; the creation of commissions to study and implement collective contracts; freedom for peasants to organise; the enactment of family allowances and other social welfare measures. This became the platform of a single national confederation, the Central Unica de Trabajadores (CUT), which was established in 1953. The Law in Defence of Democracy was not repealed until 1957 and the work of the CUT was therefore hampered, but it carried on an intense campaign for the above demands. This programme was to form the basis of the Popular Unity's election platform in the 1960s.

Before the election of Salvador Allende's Popular Unity government in 1970, Chile experienced the Christian Democratic Party's attempt to achieve a 'revolution in liberty'. President Eduardo Frei (1964-70) instituted a series of reforms which tried to tackle the country's basic problems within a capitalist framework. Some advances were made particularly in the countryside where agrarian reform and rural unionisation made some improvements in the position of the traditionally neglected peasants. However, the Christian Democrats were unable significantly to improve workers' living standards or fundamentally alter the country's inequitable social and economic structures. Opposition to the government gradually increased until in 1967

OUT! Gonzalo Lopez. Factory occupation in demand for nationalisation under Popular Unity government.

five copper miners were killed by troops during a general strike against attempts to limit the right to strike and impose a compulsory savings plan on workers. Although Frei took the unprecedented step of consulting CUT leaders on wage level adjustments for the public sector in 1970, it was a case of too little too late.

The CUT took an active part in the campaign that brought Allende to power in 1970. One of the first acts of the new government was to sign an agreement with workers' leaders accepting the participation of workers in the 'process of national transformation'. Many CUT leaders took positions in the administration of public sector industries and a start was made in putting the CUT programme into operation. Measures taken by the government ranged from the nationalisation of copper and worker participation in the managment of public sector industries to the distribution of free school milk to children under 15 and the legalisation of abortion.

The government faced serious opposition in Congress where it did not have an overall majority. The right wing parties were also active outside Congress in organising opposition to the government. The conservative social forces in Chile, in alliance with the United States, whose economic interests were at stake, combined to sabotage the Popular Unity's programme through the use of hoarding to promote artificial scarcities, the cutting of vital international credit, the secret funding and encouragement of strikes by professional groups and lorry drivers, a propaganda campaign through the conservative-controlled press and a series of other measures designed to destabilise the government. The effects of this strategy added to the inevitable short term difficulties caused by attempts to reorganise the economy for the benefit of working people and led to an increase in inflation and a serious economic crisis. Nevertheless, support for the government within the working class and peasantry increased. In reply to conservative-sponsored disruption of the economy, new forms of organisation began to appear known as 'cordones industriales' which linked factories through workers' committees which controlled production and distribution.

Faced with the mobilisation of working people and the continuing popularity of the government, the dominant classes played their trump card. On 11 September 1973, the navy occupied Valparaiso, the airforce bombed the Presidential

Palace and the army rounded up opposition leaders and trade unionists in a bloody coup which, at a stroke, wiped out the gains of the labour movement and the left wing political parties. The CUT was dissolved, unions were put under government control and all political parties banned. A military junta headed by General Augusto Pinochet took power and began the political and economic policies which were to make Chile an international byword for repression and provoke an unprecedented wave of trade union solidarity throughout the world.

Faced with savage persecution and the implementation of an economic policy which has resulted in massive unemployment and a sharp decline in real wages, the labour movement has faced the greatest difficulties in reorganising. However, govern-ment attempts to create an alternative central labour organisation have failed while unions have been partially successful in forging new organs of unity such as the Trade Union Defence Command formed in 1979.

In addition to the physical elimination of known leaders and militants, and the impoverishment of the vast mass of workers, the junta has introduced legislation aimed at creating a powerless and atomised trade union movement. A 1978 decree that adversely affected job security, minimum wage levels, and working conditions in the countryside laid the ground for the all-embracing 1979 labour code.

In addition to these decrees, the junta has outlawed independent union groupings such as the National Trade Union Coordination (CNS) and forced union elections aimed at eliminating experienced and authentic leadership. Workers replied by writing in the names of famous comedians, assassinated union leaders and disappeared prisoners on their voting forms.

The strikes of late 1979 and early 1980, and particularly that of the *El Teniente* copper workers are clear signs of a recovery of confidence but six years after the most infamous coup in modern Latin American history, the Chilean labour movement still remains weak and unable to launch a major challenge on the military's grip on the country. Gains that have taken a century of struggle have been wiped out by the army, by a social and economic elite whose privileges were under attack, and a 'free market' monetarist economic policy admired by many in the British Conservative Party.

Chilean peasants during the Allende government's agrarian reform programme.

COLOMBIA

POPULATION	25.9 million
ECON. ACTIVE	7.7 million
UNIONISED	20%
UNEMPOLOYED	13%
LIFE EXPECTANCY	63.4 years

CONFEDERATIONS

CGT — Confederacion General de Trabajadores (1971). Affil. CLAT. 70,000 members in 57 unions. Calle 17, 10-68, Piso 2, Bogota.

CSTC — Confederacion Sindical de Trabajadores de Colombia (1964). Affil. CPUSTAL. 300,000 members in 35 industrial federations including beer, cement, textiles, transport, metal.
Carrera 14, 15-42, Bogota.

CTC — Central de Trabajadores de Colombia (1936). Affil. ORIT. 350,000 members with federations in 25 departments. Strong in ports, sugar and transport. Close to Liberal Party.
Calle 16, 13-14, Bogota.

UTC — Union de Trabajadores de Colombia (1946). Affil. ORIT. Claims 800,000 members. Federations in all departments and most industries, particularly strong amongst textile and metal workers. Close to Conservative Party.
Carrera 10, 7-33, Bogota.

MAJOR UNIONS

Federacion de Trabajadores de las Industrias Metalurgicas, Electricas y Mecanicas (metal and electricity workers). 10,000 members.
Calle 16, 16-22, Bogota.

Federacion Nacional de Choferes y Asalariados del Transporte (drivers).
Calle 16, 14-13, Piso 5, Bogota.

Federacion Nacional de Sindicatos Bancarios (bank workers).
Calle 14, 12-50, Oficina 615, Bogota.

Federacion Nacional de Trabajadores de la Construccion (construction workers).
Avenida Caracas, 15-42, Bogota.

Union de Trabajadores Metalurgicos y Mineros (metal and mine workers). 25,000 members.
Carrera 8a, 3-56, Bogota.

INDEPENDENT UNIONS

ACEB — Asociacion Colombiana de Empleados Bancarios (bank workers).

CITE — Comite Intersindical de Trabajadores del Estado (state employees).

FECODE — Federacion Colombiana de Educadores (teachers).

FENALTRASE — Federacion Nacional de Trabajadores al Servicio del Estado (state employees). Unification with CITE announced but not yet effective.
Edificio Santa Fe, Carrera A6, 14-12, Oficina 330, Bogota.

SITTELECOM — Sindicato de Trabajadores de Telecomunicaciones de Colombia (telecommunications workers).

USO — Union Sindical Obrera (oil workers).

The first major strikes by organised labour occurred in 1918 and 1919 when railwaymen and then dockers won wage increases. These years also saw the first attempts to organise workers at a national level, and in 1919, a well-attended workers' congress took place. Although the congress set its sights on developing mutual benefits and obtaining political representation for the labour movement, it was a series of long bitter strikes against United States transnational companies which dominated the 1920s.

Discontent with working conditions triggered a strike at the Tropical Oil Company in 1924. Faced with the company's refusal to negotiate, the workers rebelled and took control of the local town in what became known as the Barrancabermeja Commune. But the workers made minimal gains, and mass sackings followed the end of the strike. When events repeated themselves three years later, the government passed a law allowing companies to sack all workers involved in union activities.

Following a major strike on the banana plantations of the United Fruit Company in 1928 the government declared a state of siege and the army fired on a crowd of demonstrators, killing hundreds of men, women and children. This event, known as the 'Massacre of the Banana Workers', was a landmark in the history of the Colombian labour movement.

Labour unrest, the growth of socialist influence, and the emergence of populist political figures such as Jorge Eliecer Gaitan, propelled the traditional Liberal Party into calling for reforms. The Liberals came to power in the 1930 presidential election and the following year trade unions were officially granted the right to organise. The government of President Alfonso Lopez (1934-38) saw great strides in the development of the labour movement. Comprehensive labour legislation was introduced and all workers apart from public employees were given the right to strike. Many individual unions were formed in these years and in 1936, the Confederation of Workers of Colombia (CTC) was established, uniting the powerful oil, rail and river workers' federations, and a considerable number of industrial and professional unions.

The victory of the Conservatives in 1938 reversed what progress the labour movement had made, but the re-election of Lopez in 1942 gave another impetus to trade union development. In 1945 government decrees established minimum wage regulations, paid holidays and overtime pay. To combat victimisation, union officials were granted job security and safeguards against strike breaking were introduced. However, the division of the Liberal Party led to a Conservative victory in the 1946 election; the recent gains made by Labour were wiped out, and the attempt by the CTC to topple the government by a general strike failed.

Riots in Bogota following the murder of Gaitan in 1948 led to an intermittent civil war which lasted almost a decade and cost the lives of thousands of Colombians. This period in Colombian history is simply known as 'La Violencia'. Years of authoritarian rule under Presidents Ospina Perez, Gomez and Rojas Pinilla left the labour movement in disarray. The CTC was virtually obliterated, but the Union of Workers of Colombia (UTC) established by the Conservative Party to counter the influence of the Liberal-dominated CTC, made progress, receiving the backing of successive Colombian governments and the United States.

Although President Rojas Pinilla (1953-57) promised to respect trade union rights and allowed the CTC to re-open its national offices, he tried to establish a central labour organisation completely loyal to himself, and ended by alienating even the conservative UTC. When Rojas Pinilla tried to stay in office for a second term, he was forced into exile by an alliance of the Liberal and Conservative Parties. In one of the most enduring political arrangements of recent Latin American history, these two parties, representing different factions of the dominant class, agreed to share power for a period of 16 years. This arrangement still continues though on a more informal basis. They gained a firm grip on the bureaucracies of the CTC and the UTC, and apart from brief periods of labour unrest, they have controlled them ever since. A survey carried out in 1971 showed that 71% of workers felt neither the Conservatives or the Liberals represented their interests, yet their unions continue to be affiliated to the CTC and UTC.

The late 1950s and early 1960s saw workers' real wages increase, and unions forced concessions from the government of President Valencia with the threat of a general strike in 1965. However, workers' living standards and rights have been constantly under pressure. In 1966, the right to strike was restricted by the imposition of arbitration procedures after 40 days. Further plans by President Lleras Restrepo (1966-70) were blocked by worker opposition, and pressure from the rank and file forced the UTC and CTC to take up a position critical of the government. An increase in public transport fares provoked violent demonstrations, with the government threatening to suspend legal recognition of those unions who opposed the move, but eventually a compromise was reached.

The 1960s saw the emergence of the Trade Union Confederation of Workers of Colombia (CSTC) and other independent unions which helped to break down the monopoly of the government-controlled confederations. The CSTC has grown steadily and is now the second largest confederation.

The early 1970s was a period of relative calm, but as inflation accelerated during the presidency of Lopez Michelsen (1974-78), workers mobilised to defend their living standards. It has been calculated that real wages fell by 22.6% between 1970 and 1977. Meanwhile in the countryside, the National Association of Peasant Road Users (ANUC), originally set up by the government in 1970, organised the peasants to take over land on the large rural estates which led to fierce repression from landowners and the army.

A high point in labour militancy came in 1977 with a series of major strikes. The Oil Workers Union (USO) struck after the state oil company ECOPETROL failed to honour a collective agreement. The government intervened by suspending the union and sending in troops to occupy ECOPETROL installations. A strike of 2,500 agricultural workers at the Indupalma plantation, and the unprecedented solidarity from other unions and individuals and the kidnapping of the company's managing director by guerillas forced the company to comply with minimum wage legislation, respect the eight-hour day, re-instate those sacked at the beginning of the dispute and draw up workers' contracts, thus making the firm responsible for welfare benefits. A long teachers' strike by the powerful independent union FECODE ended in compromise.

The death of more than a hundred coal miners in an explosion at the Villa Diana mine at Amaga demonstrated the dangerous working conditions to which many industrial workers are subjected; a recent report by the International Labour Organisation also spotlighted the use of child labour in Colombian coal mines.

Labour unrest led to a general strike in September 1977 after the government failed to meet claims for a national wage rise. The government's intransigence and pressure from rank and file union members led the UTC and CTC into joining the General Confederation of Workers (CGT) and CSTC in a 24 hour

consistently refused to deal with the CGT and CSTC which he characterises as 'extremist'. Although all the confederations have combined to commemorate the anniversary of the general strike and a National Trade Union Council (CNS) has been established, unity is extremely fragile.

The government's attitude to the labour movement is indicated by its consistent refusal fully to comply with ILO accords 87 and 98 on the freedom to organise, even though the national minister gave the remarkable reply that the ratification only committed Colombia at an international level and did not mean that the accords had automatic validity inside the country. The government has habitually arrested union leaders, frozen union funds, and suspended their legal status as a means of breaking strikes. The introduction of the Security Statute in 1978 consolidated and extended this suppression of democratic rights and has placed the labour movement

national protest strike. They demanded a 50% general pay rise, the freezing of prices and public service charges, a definitive lifting of the state of siege, the re-opening and demilitarisation of the universities, full trade union rights for all state sector workers, land for the peasants and an end to repression in the countryside, an eight-hour working day and application of minimum wage legislation for transport workers, and the abolition of the decrees which reorganised the Colombian Institute for Social Security to the detriment of the users and workers of that organisation.

The government replied by sending troops on to the streets. Eighteen people were killed and several thousand arrests were made. The government's declaration of a 26% increase in the minimum wage and the ambiguous position of the CTC and UTC helped to defuse tension and divide the labour movement. The government of President Turbay (1978-) has

and all opposition to the democratic rights and has placed the labour movement and all opposition to the government under further pressure.

UNION SINDICAL OBRERA (USO)

The Union Sindical Obrera, the oil workers' union, has long been in the vanguard of the Colombian labour movement. The union was secretly organised in 1922 and led the struggles against the oil companies in the 1920s. The union was officially recognised in 1938, but soon after a strike resulted in the massacre of many workers. Oil was nationalised in 1948 after a nationwide campaign led by the striking oil workers against the renewal of the transnational concessions. During 1979 USO carried out a national campaign in opposition to the policies of ECOPETROL, the state oil company. The last major strike by USO took place towards the end of 1977 when the union was suspended by the government and troops sent to occupy ECOPETROL installations. Support for the workers in the major oil town, Barrancabermeja, and the survival of the union in clandestinity allowed the union to gain some of its objectives, but it failed to stop production completely or negotiate the reinstatement of more than 200 sacked workers.

In spite of intimidation and harassment by government and employers, the union eventually won a 24% pay rise, a promise by the company to build a hospital for the workers and company commitments to contribute a further 40 million pesos towards housing workers. USO has taken a leading role in moves to unite the independent unions around common objectives. It organised a national meeting for this purpose in January 1980.

COSTA RICA

POPULATION	2.0 million
ECON. ACTIVE	700,000
UNIONISED	
UNEMPLOYED	4.6%
LIFE EXPECTANCY	71.8 years

CONFEDERATIONS

CATD — Central Autentica de Trabajadores Democraticos (1978) Independent.

CCTD — Confederacion Costarricense de Trabajadores Democraticos (1943) Affil. ORIT. Calle Central, Avenida 5-7, Apartado 2167, San Jose.

CGT — Confederacion General de Trabajadores (1953) Affil. CPUSTAL Includes UTG — Union de Trabajadores del Golfito. Calles 10-12, Avenida 20, Apartado 1039, San Jose.

MAJOR UNIONS

ANE — Asociacion Nacional de Educadores (teachers) 18,000 Apartado 2938, San Jose.

FENATRAP — Federacion Nacional de Trabajadores Publicos. Includes ANEP (government administration), ICE (electricity workers) and other public sector workers.

Sindicato Industrial de Trabajadores Textiles (textile workers) Apartado 2167, Casa Paraiso, San Jose.

Union de Trabajadores Bananeros del Atlantico (banana workers) Apartado 539, Puerto Limon.

This small Central American country has achieved a degree of political liberalism in a region traditionally dominated by military dictatorships. There is a relatively comprehensive welfare system and a reasonable standard of education — Costa Rica has the highest literacy level in Central America at 86%. However, recently a deepening economic crisis has increased labour unrest.

In 1905, the Federation of Artisans, Bakers, Construction Workers and Carpenters was formed to be followed three years later by the Mutualist society of Print Workers. Soon afterwards the General Confederation of Workers was founded which, in 1921, promoted a general strike that succeeded in forcing a 40% pay rise throughout the country, and the recognition of the eight hour day.

The 1930s was a time of intense organisation and major strikes. Labour unrest was centred on the plantations of the United Fruit Company. In 1932, 10,000 banana and port workers went on strike paralysing the port of Puntarenas for several days. Although troops were called in to break the strike, the workers secured the recognition of some trade union rights. However, it was not until the presidency of Rafael Calderon Guardia (1940-43) that workers were given substantial freedom to organise. A comprehensive labour was introduced in 1943 and a ministry of labour and social welfare was established. This code and a section of the 1949 Constitution form the labour legislation currently in force.

In the early 1940s, the Communist Party established the Confederation of Costa Rican Workers (CTCR) grouping 96 individual unions and, in 1943, the church sponsored the creation of the Costa Rican Confederation of Workers (CCT), now the Costa Rican Confederation of Democratic Workers (CCTD).

A period of political instability in the mid-1940s resulted in a brief but violent civil war. The victors took the remarkable step of abolishing the army, but its role is effectively played by a powerful Civil Guard. The 1950s was a time of relative peace on the labour front. The General Confederation of Workers (CGT), re-constituted from the outlawed CTCR, grew in strength as the CCT declined, but the degree of organisation of the working class was generally weak. Although the United Fruit Company was involved in various attempts to dissolve and weaken the plantation workers' union — there were no strikes in 1962, 1963 or 1966 — all disputes were settled peacefully through the labour courts.

In recent years the economy has grown at a faster rate and the workforce has become more concentrated. There has been greater labour unrest and a corresponding growth in the size and influence of worker organisations. Several major disputes have taken place since 1978. In September 1978, a ten day strike by 18,000 hospital workers ended with a wage rise but defeat for the workers' other central demand — free collective bargaining. The trade union rights of public employees are limited in law. The major confederations supported the strike with the notable exception of the CCDT.

In February 1979, the workers of the United Brands subsidiary (formerly United Fruit) won a decisive victory by gaining a wage increase of 30%. The settlement was worked out by an official mediator who even backdated the pay rise by two months. Although

Nicaraguan refugees in Costa Rica during the insurrection against Somoza.

the strike was at first declared illegal by the local labour court, the government was forced to handle the situation sympathetically. The eventual settlement discredited the labour courts, not known for their impartiality. Most of the 4,000 workers involved belonged to the Union of Workers of Golfito (UTG), the most militant union in the country.

August 1979 witnessed serious labour unrest in the Atlantic port of Limon. The port, oil refineries, railway and major public and private companies were brought to a standstill by workers claiming higher wages and improved working conditions. The strike was organised by the most powerful regional federation in the country — the Federation of Workers of Limon (FETRAL). When the government and employers flew in strikebreakers, tension increased and there were clashes with the police. Eventually, the government allowed a settlement satisfactory to the workers. The labour minister was dismissed and her replacement said that, 'in the future, there will be a policy of dialogue' with the union. This, however, has scarcely proved to be the case.

Much of the recent unrest has been caused by increases in the rate of inflation; Costa Rica imports all its oil and it has been badly hit by the energy crisis. In addition, the Nicaraguan civil war had adverse effects on the country's economy in that it led to the cutting of road links with the rest of Central America and Mexico. In 1979, there were major strikes by teachers, public sector employees and the important banana workers. Although these were not repressed to a degree normal in Central America, the police were widely used and many workers injured — an indication of the difficulties the labour movement is likely to face in the future.

CUBA

POPULATION	10 million
EC. ACTIVE	5.6 million
UNIONISED	
UNEMPLOYED	
LIFE EXPECTANCY	70 years (1975)

CONFEDERATION

CTC — Confederacion de Trabadores Cubanos (1939). Affil. CPUSTAL. Membership of over two million, includes all national unions. Placio de los Trabajadores, Penalver y San Carlos, Havana.

The first union in Cuba was that of the tobacco workers, founded in 1868, and shortly followed by several artisanal mutualist societies. In 1883, a 'workers' circle' was established in the capital Havana and in 1892 the first national workers' congress took place, raising demands for independence from Spain and the eight hour day. However, after the war of 1898-99 Cuba fell under US control and it was not until 1920 that the militant railwaymen's union was able to win the eight hour day and help establish a union for the sugar workers that comprised the bulk of the proletariat.

Being dependent upon a single crop-sugar-the Cuban economy suffered badly from major fluctuations in the world market and was severely hit following the recovery of the European beet fields after the First World War. In order to maintain a tight hold upon a population that was becoming more radical in the face of this crisis the US sanctioned the harsh dictatorship of General Machado. But when Cuba was hit by the full force of the depression in the early 1930s Machado was unable to maintain control through repression and was overthrown in 1933 after a busworkers' strike had developed into a general stoppage and ncos mutinied against the officer corps. There followed a succession of short-lived progressive regimes that enabled the labour movement to strengthen and develop but when, in March 1935, the new army chief General Fulgencio Batista moved to clamp down on this process a second general strike was ruthlessly suppressed with hundreds jailed and thousands, mostly sugar workers, put out of work.

It took three years for the unions to reorganise and it was not until January 1939 that the Cuban Workers Confederation (CTC) was established amidst considerable internal conflict. At first the CTC was controlled by the Communist Party (PSP) which briefly collaborated with Batista in the liberal phase of his government following the introduction of the 1940 Constitution. However, the PSP lost control in the mid-1940s at the outset of the Cold War.

In 1952, Batista returned to power through a coup and once again established a dictatorial regime, dispensing with the Constitution. At first the CTC called for a general strike but Batista was able to buy off the bueaucracy with a promise to respect union rights. Consequently the next two congresses, in 1953 and 1956, were held under government surveillance and direction.

At this time Fidel Castro's guerila campaign in the Sierra Maestra was beginning to have an impact, and as the regime became increasingly embattled many prominent union leaders joined the urban underground

US guard of honour for President Batista of Cuba, 1942.

resistance movement which played an important but often neglected role in the Revolution. Inside the CTC this opposition was headed not by the communists but by Catholic radicals and liberals who, by and large, supported the guerillas and following the overthrow of Batista in January 1959 the leadership of the CTC lay in the hands of those who backed Castro. But he yet to declare himself a marxist.

The CTC elections in late 1959 resulted in a decisive defeat for the PSP and the new government was forced to intervene directly and impose 'unity', backing up the ailing PSP forces and purging those who opposed this. In May 1960, the general secretary of the CTC, David Salvador, was jailed and at the 11th national congress only one list of candidates for office was presented with the veteran PSP member Lazaro Pena, who had been general secretary from 1939 to 1947) replacing Salvador and staying in office until 1966.

Following the US blockade established in 1961 and the abortive CIA-backed 'Bay of Pigs' invasion, Cuba turned to the Soviet Union and embarked upon wholesale socialisation of the economy. This naturally entailed an entirely new role for the unions which had hitherto practised a quite highly developed system of collective bargaining. This was brought to an end in December 1959, and in 1961 a new legal system was introduced for labour codifying and expanding the premise laid down by Che Guevara: 'The Cuban workers have to get used to living in a collectivist regime and, therefore, cannot strike.' The logic of this being that since Cuba was now a workers' state it was impossible for workers to strike against themselves.

In 1966, the 12th congress of the CTC approved a Declaration of Principles which stated that the labour movement, directed and guided by the party, must effectively contribute to the mobilisation of the masses in fulfillment of the tasks assigned by the Revolution and to the strengthening of marxism-leninism.' The principal tasks of the unions were outlined as assisting in increasing output and efficiency, expanding social facilities, improving political education and the application of work quotas, wage scales and labour discipline. They were not to intervene in the formulation of production plans which were reserved exclusively for management. Moreover, the unions were not responsible for policy decisions concerning working conditions or legislation.

By the mid-1960s, 1.5 million of the 1.9 million eligible for membership were unionised, only the police, private farmers and the army were banned from

Cubans celebrate the Bay of Pigs victory.

membership. After 1965, many of the traditional functions of the unions passed to elected 'labour councils' set up in the workplace with limited supervisory powers. Nevertheless, administrators still retained broad disciplinary powers that enabled them to sack workers without reference to the councils or union.

For most of the 1960s the Cuban economy was run with workers subject to 'moral' rather than 'material' incentives and wages were set by the ministry of labour according to four major scales, each containing seven or eight grades. Thus, in 1965 grade 1 of scale 1, agricultural workers, received 64 pesos per month whilst grade 7 received 154 pesos; grade 1 of scale 2, non-agricultural workers, received 85 pesos with grade 8 in receipt of 264. the uppermost wage was roughly fifteen times the lowest. In the face of over twenty years of diplomatic and economic warefare from the US it is scarcely surprising that Cuba has had to resort to a siege economy for long periods: wages are low and state rationing of all basic commodities remains very tight indeed, but Cuban workers benefit from the best health, social service and educational facilities in Latin America as a result of socialist planning.

After the failure of Castro's campaign for a ten million ton sugar harvest in 1970 major alterations were made in economic planning including the progressive introduction of material incentives and the development of a small parallel 'black' market to offset the austerities bred by rationing. At the same time the government leadership berated the CTC for its lack of democracy, but since the CTC had very little independence from the government itself this was in effect open self-criticism, spurred on by grow-

One of Cuba's main economic problems has been its reliance on sugar and tobacco, now it is trying to diversify into industrial production.

ing discontent among rank and file workers. However, there was no national congress between 1966 and 1974 and only in 1971 did union elections take place on a national scale.

At its 13th congress in 1974 the CTC ratified the official policy of tying wage rates to productivity but at the 14th congress in 1978 this came in for much criticism since in many instances it was plain that a fall in output had little to do with the workers yet they suffered a loss in wages as a result. There was also criticism of the work quotas and production levels. Allied to this the very high level of participation in the union elections of 1978 suggested that ordinary workers were beginning to take a more direct part in union affairs, even though these remained closely circumscribed by the dictates of the government.

The limited role ordained for

The revolution has brought an educational system that starts at kindergarten, something rarely found in other Latin American countries.

the unions in Cuba is not simply the product of the socialisation of the means of production, it is also officially justified by the existence of other organs for popular participation in decision-making, most notably the local assemblies and the national assembly — the 'supreme organ of state power' — linked through the system known as *Poder Popular* ('Popular Power'), established in 1974. It is, however, evident that while this has increased democracy in decision-making at local level the assemblies have very little independence from the bureaucratic hierarchy and are far more concerned with specific administrative issues than with questions of policy. In fact, as the economy has run into further difficulties — as a result of low sugar prices, lack of foreign exchange, the failure of the tobacco crop in 1979-80 and the continued US boycott on trade — the response has not been to increase democracy by incorporating decisions made on the shopfloor or in the fields but rather a greater bureaucratisation.

Moreover, in the face of one of the worst economic crises since 1959 there has been a qualitative shift away from the economic model of the 1960s to the requirement that state enterprises show a profit, thereby increasing the level of unemployment, and to the relaxation of the state monopoly on retailing as well as of the strict regulation of wage levels, the defence of which Castro has called 'petty bourgeois egalitarianism'. This new turn contributed to the extensive unrest apparent at the end of 1979 and early in 1980, with Castro responding by increasing the police presence in the major cities and taking over three ministries personally — a centralisation of power that runs against the ethos of *poder popular*.

The degree to which discontent has been exacerbated by the economic measures was to some extent evident in the mass exodus of over 100,000 Cubans to the US and Latin American countries between April and June 1980. While the US naturally made a great deal of publicity over the refugee campaign and likened it to the fate of the Vietnamese boat people, the Cuban government asserted that the vast majority were 'degenerate elements, homosexuals, vagrants and traitors'. There can be little doubt that such people were among the refugees — homosexuals in particular are vilified in Cuba — but it is highly likely that a great number of those who left the island were ordinary working people lured away from the austerity of the isolated socialist state by the promise of affluence proffered by the US. For many such illusions were shattered very quickly after their arrival, as evidenced by the riots in the reception camps.

Nevertheless, the refugee issue marked a resumption by the US of many of the policies of the Cold War era following the Soviet invasion of Afghanistan, bringing to an end the diplomatic overtures and gradual relaxation of the economic blockade. The effects of this on Cuban workers will be substantial; for them a period of renewed hardship seems inevitable and the struggle for full political participation as important as ever.

DOMINICAN REPUBLIC

POPULATION	5.3 million
ECON. ACTIVE	1.6 million
UNIONISED	
UNEMPLOYED	40% (1978)
LIFE EXPECTANCY	61.2 years

CONFEDERATIONS

CASC — Confederacion Autonoma Sindical Clasista (formerly Cristiana) (1978). Affil. CLAT.
Apartado 309, Juan Erazo 35237, Santo Domingo.

CGT — Confederacion General de Trabajadores (1972, recognised 1974). Groups 50 unions, including FUTA (food and hotel workers), ADP (teachers), SINOMAPE (heavy machinery operators) plus regional federations. Cooperates with independents, including UNACHOSIN (drivers), POASI (dockers), SIT (telephone workers) and SITRACODE (electrical workers).
Calle Paris 65, Santo Domingo.
European Bureau: Fernando de la Rosa, c/o OTT, 111, rue des Rabats, 92160 Antony, France.

UGTD — Union General de Trabajadores Dominicanos (1978). Government-backed.

The first important labour organisation in the Dominican Republic was the Local Federation of Labour, established in 1916. This fought for better conditions and against the occupation of the island by US marines between 1916 and 1924. The first national confederation was the Dominican Confederation of Labour (CDT) established in the 1920s which was later turned into a government agency by the Trujillo dictatorship (1930-61). Throughout this period, there was no significant authentic trade union activity apart from a brief interlude just after the Second World War. In 1946, Mauricio Baez led a sugar workers' strike supported by all the unions in the region of San Pedro de Macoris. Trujillo clamped down and Baez was arrested, tortured, and several years later he was murdered. Throughout the 1950s, the repression of the labour movement was condemned by the ICFTU and even the AFL-CIO. In 1957, a delegation from the AFL-CIO and the Cuban CTC visited the Dominican Republic. They concluded that there was neither collective bargaining nor genuine trade unions in the country, and found evidence of the existence of some forced labour. The assassination of Trujillo in 1961 sparked off a wave of organisation in the labour movement. The United Labour Front for Autonomous Trade Unions (FOUPSA) was established in 1961. From this came the FOUPSA Libre which in 1962 changed its name to National Confederation of Free Workers (CONATRAL, aff. ORIT). Another group broke away from FOUPSA to form the Trade Union Confederation of Dominican Workers (CESITRADO). In 1962, the Autonomous Christian Trade Union Confederation (CASC) was also formed. It became second in size to CONATRAL.

CONATRAL was financed and organised by the United States to oppose the reformist government of President Juan Bosch. In July 1963, Ruiz Lopez, leader of CONATRAL, publicly called on the army to follow the example recently set by the Ecuadorian armed forces (i.e. overthrow the constitutional government). Bosch was in fact overthrown and the army under Donald Reid Cabral took over (1963-65). A popular movement to restore the constitutional government was broken when the United States invaded the country and placed the right wing Joaquin Balaguer in power. CONATRAL remained a government agency but underwent a rapid decline as it completely lost touch with the workers.

Strike breaking, the prohibition of union demonstration, jailing and exile of union leaders, the formation of company unions and the outlawing of independent worker organisations were all features of the Balaguer regime. However, labour continued to organise at grass roots level and there was considerable unrest at the beginning of the 1970s when the government imposed a wage freeze at a time of high inflation. One product of this activity was the formation of the General Confederation of Workers (CGT) in 1972 by unions independent of the

CGT poster puts forward the sugar workers' demand for freedom, equal wages and unity; above—Tate and Lyle sugar refinery.

March 1979. This congress resolved to promote unity in the labour movement and to fight for a new labour code, the right of free organisation, the reform of the social security laws and the definitive right to strike.

In April 1979, a national congress of peasants called for land reform, state control of large foreign owned estates, nationalisation of transnational agricultural enterprises, the elimination of intermediaries in the marketing of agricultural produce, minimum wage legislation and social security provisions for the peasantry.

The government has raised the minimum wage to 125 Dominican dollars per month but a family of six needs 113.12 for food alone. The high cost of basic commodities sparked off riots in Santo Domingo in August 1979 when taxi drivers (who provide the basic means of transport in the capital) protested against the increase in petrol prices. The Hurricane David disaster in 1979 to some extent covered up the government's failure to meet its promises. One other consequence of the hurricane was that employers took the opportunity to lay off workers, picking on the most militant in the union movement, on the grounds of shortage of materials and other similar pretexts. Although the government promised to stop this practice, it has failed to do anything about it. The unions have been very active in the months since the hurricane and a union committee set up to participate in the reconstruction of the country drew up plans to aid the population most affected by the disaster. However, the independent labour movement faces the prospect of a continuing struggle to retain its independence and a difficult fight to maintain workers' living standards.

Elections in 1978 ended the repressive Balaguer regime with a victory for the Dominican Revolutionary Party (PRD). A wave of unionisation followed and 118 new unions were officially registered between August 1978 and February 1979. Scattered strikes achieved some concessions on wages and working conditions but the employers have maintained their stance even if the government has changed. In addition, the PRD has attempted to impede the creation of strong independent trade unions. The government has set up the General Union of Dominican Workers (UGTD) in an attempt to exercise close control over the unions, and although it has nationalised some major United States transnationals like Rosario Mining, its economic policies are not substantially different from those of the Balaguer government. The CGT has nevertheless continued its progress and held its first national congress in

government. The CGT has, however, suffered constant harassment in common with its affiliates. One example of this occurred in September 1974 when the Dominican Oil Refinery, a subsidiary of Shell, cancelled its union contract and fired union leaders on charges of inciting a work stoppage while the police attacked the CGT offices making many arrests.

ECUADOR

POPULATION	7.1 million
ECON. ACTIVE	2.2 million
UNIONISED	22% (ALAI 1977)
UNEMPLOYED	44% (including underemployment – LANL)
LIFE EXPECTANCY	62.1 years

CONFEDERATIONS

CEDOC – Central Ecuatoriana de Organizaciones Clasistas (1976). Independent. Main affiliate: FENOC – Federacion Nacional de Organizaciones Campesinas (peasants) comprising about 80% of the total CEDOC membership.

CEDOC de los Trabajadores (1976). Affil. CLAT.

CEDOC was originally established in 1938 and had a membership of 37,500 in 1973. The organisation split in 1976 with the more radical group leaving CLAT but retaining the original name.

CEOSL – Confederacion Ecuatoriana de Organizaciones Sindicales Libres (1962). Affil. ORIT. 32,500 members.

CTE – Confederacion de Trabajadores del Ecuador (1944). Affil. CPUSTAL. 40,000 members.
Controls FEI – Federacion Ecuatoriana de Indios (peasants).

INDEPENDENTS

There are some 2,200 independent unions with 110,000 members.

The first workers' societies were formed around the turn of the century in the port of Guayaquil. The first important labour organisations were the Labour Confederation of Guayas (1905) and the Catholic Centre of Workers (1908). The first struggles centered around demands for higher wages and shorter working hours and, in 1916, a law was passed establishing the eight-hour day although it was largely ignored by employers.

In 1920, in the aftermath of the important railwaymen's strike of 1919, the second national workers' congress was held. It called for the government to protect workers' interests and establish a ministry of social welfare. Militancy increased with industrial action by railwaymen and dockers in 1920 and 1922, the regime of the time replying with a massacre of over 500 workers at a demonstration in 1922. Pressure from the working class forced recognition of the right to join unions and to strike in the 1928 Constitution. Further action in 1934, when there was a series of strikes throughout the country in demand of minimum wage legislation, regulation of child and female labour, overtime pay and employer recognition of the eight hour day, helped to create the political climate in which the first comprehensive code was passed (1938).

The first important national union confederation, the Ecuadorian Confederation of Catholic Workers (CEDOC), was set up in 1938 under the strong influence of the Catholic church. The conservatism of the CEDOC's sponsors and the fact that many of the affiliates were artisanal groups meant that the confederation did not at first play a significant role in the advance of the labour movement. The establishment of the Confederation of Workers of Ecuador (CTE) in 1944 with the participation of most industrial unions did, however, provide a more radical focus for organisation. Although weakened under the military dictatorship of 1963-66, the CTE has remained a powerful body; numerically it is the largest of the three national confederations and remains most significant in the industrial and service sector.

CEDOC, meanwhile, began to move away from its close identification with the church. After its 1955 congress, and under the leadership of a metal worker, Humberto Valdez, it began to recruit more industrial workers. In the 1960s it took a lead in organising rural workers and established the National Federation of Peasant Organisations (FENOC). The third major labour confederation, the Ecuadorian Confederation of Free Trade Union Organisations (CEOSL) was formed in 1962 by US labour organisers and reactionary political forces precisely to undermine the growing militancy and popularity of CEDOC and the CTE. US intelligence played an important role in this as former CIA agent Phillip Agee testified in his book *CIA Diary*; 'CEOSL is founded with several agents in key posts. There was a considerable publicity campaign with messages of solidarity from ORIT in Mexico, from ICFTU, and the international secretariat in Brussels.'

The labour movement suffered a major setback in 1963 when the military took power in a coup. In 1966, after mounting political pressure and working class militancy, the army was forced out and the right to strike restored. By the end of 1969 the three confederations had

established a common position on basic demands and this trend towards unity was consolidated during the civilian dictatorship of Velasco Ibarra (1970-72) when the CTE and CEDOC joined forces in the United Front of Workers (FUT). A general strike was called in July 1971 but the government jailed the leadership of both confederations, passed anti-strike legislation and imposed mass sackings.

In 1972 the military took over again under the leadership of General Rodriguez Lara. This regime attempted to consolidate itself with a radical nationalist programme and much populist rhetoric but failed to realise these and offered very little to the working class. When Rodriguez Lara was removed by reactionary officers in 1976 the government returned to the traditional anti-labour stance of the military. The move towards unity within the union move-

ment was given further impetus under these adverse circumstances but considerable divisions still remained.

At its national congress in 1972 CEDOC cast off completely its identification with the church, changing its name to the Ecuadorian Confederation of Class Organisations and calling for major structural reforms in Ecuadorean society. In 1974 the three confederations called jointly for agrarian reform, nationalisation of the oil industry, the banning of imports of luxury items and the extension of social security to the peasants. In 1975 they adopted an action programme of nine points and called a national strike in support of these demands.

However, in May 1976 CEDOC split when CLAT, in alliance with the more reactionary elements of the national leadership, forced the departure of the radicals who took the majority of the member-

ship and retained the support of FENOC. It was the followers of CLAT, however, that changed their name — to CEDOC de los Trabajadores (The Workers' CEDOC).

Unity between the confederations was, nevertheless, consolidated for a while at least in the general strike of May 1977 when 150,000 workers and peasants called for the immediate resolution of all conflicts, full rights to strike and organise, a 50% wage increase and the establishment of a sliding scale of wages linked to inflation. Demands were also made for the nationalisation of the oil and electrical industries, the implementation of the oil and electrical industries, the implementation of agrarian reform laws, state control of foreign trade and the nationalisation of all basic necessities. The National Teachers Union (UNE) went on strike simultaneously but this widespread mobilisation was met with heavy repression. National officials and strike leaders were imprisoned and a government decree gave the police the power to try and sentence strikers without right of appeal. The aim of the regime was clearly to destroy the unity within the union movement. CEOSL, which under pressure from the rank and file had begun to adopt a more militant stance, was brought back under the control of reaction-

ary leaders. The suppression of the general strike in May was followed in October by the killing of 120 sugar workers at the Aztra mill when police attacked a demonstration. 1977 was the highest point in the repression of the labour movement but pressure for constitutional government was growing in the face of this and the army's failure to solve the country's economic crisis.

Nine years of dictatorship were brought to an end in June 1979 with the election of the social democrat Jaime Roldos. Though Roldos promised the introduction of major social reforms he has been prevented from implementing these by the conservative major-ity in congress. Nevertheless, trade union rights were confirmed, the minimum wage doubled, and the ministry of labour met with some success in defusing conflict: of the 86 industrial disputes that took place between August and November 1979 33 were solved with government intervention and only three strikes took place.

In June 1979 CEDOC presided over a 'Congress of Non-Affiliated Trade Union Organisations' which was attended by the Guatemalan CNT, the Salvadorean CCS, and the CGT from the Dominican Republic and severely criticised not only CLAT but also ORIT and CPUSTAL, calling for alternat-ive channels for international solidarity.

Of the urban unions only CEDOC de los Trabajadores made appreciable headway in 1970, benefitting from desertions from CEDOC as a result of political divisions its whole-hearted support for Roldos and solid financial support from CLAT. As Roldos attempts to impose reforms for which he has scant political backing and few economic resources the union movement remains weakened through its failure to sustain the momentum of its earlier drive for unity, a failure undoubtedly encouraged by the right wing but also helped by deep political division on the left.

Ecuadorean workers demonstrate against anti-worker legislation and 'Uncle Sam's' imperialism—May Day, 1976.

EL SALVADOR

POPULATION	4.1 million
ECON. ACTIVE	1.3 million
UNIONISED	10% (1977)
UNEMPLOYED	35% (Government figure, 1977)
LIFE EXPECTANCY	62.2 years

CONFEDERATIONS

CCS — Comite Coordinadora Sindical (1975) 29 Unions including FTC (peasants) and ANDES (teachers). Union arm of the Popular Revolutionary Bloc (BPR — Bloque Popular Revolucionario)

CGS — Confederacion General de Sindicatos (1958) Expelled from ICFTU Oct. 1979. 10,000. Three federations (textile, food and general workers) with 41 unions. Also includes SEPAS (port workers)

CNT — Confederacion Nacional de Trabajadores (2978) US and government backed. 40,000. Includes FESINCONTRANS — Federacion de Sindicatos de Construccion, Similares, Transportes y Otras (12 unions with 28,000 members) and UCS (1978) peasant union with 60,000 members, controlled by the Front for United Popular Action (FAPU).

CUTS — Confederacion Unificada de Trabajadores Salvadorenos 26,000. Three federations:

FUSS — Federacion Unificada de Sindicatos Salvadorenos (1955) Affil. CPUSTAL. 17 unions, 7,000.

FESTIAVCES — Federacion Sindical de Trabajadores de la Industria de Alimentos Vestidos y Similares de El Salvador (1968) Affil. CPUSTAL. 13 unions, 4,500.

FENASTRAS — Federacion Nacional y Sindical de Trabajadores Salvadorenos. 11 unions, 6,000. Includes important power workers union STCEL. Strong political influence of FAPU.

The first important trade union, the Society of Commercial Employees, was established in 1910. The Confederation of Workers, formed in 1914, was the first national workers' organisation, inspired by the principles and programme of the Central American Congress of Workers, which met in San Salvador in 1911.

In the 1920s many new unions were formed in the towns and countryside as workers organised themselves in pursuit of basic demands such as the eight hour day. These early unions formed the Regional Federation of Salvadorean Workers (FRTS) in 1925. The FRTS played an important role in these years, encouraging unionisation and setting up a Popular University for workers. Workers' demands contributed to a groundswell of support for political reform and at the May Day march in 1929 70,000 workers demonstrated in the capital which at the time had a population of only 100,000. A major aim of the FRTS was to pressure the government into drawing up a labour code, recognising trade union rights in law but the regime replied with repression. Social conflict sharpened as the world depression caused a deterioration in the market for Salvadorean raw materials, particularly coffee. Tension reached a peak in 1932 when the communist party-led rural rebellion ended in the massacre of some 20,000 peasants and the banning of all trade unions. This massacre still lives on in the collective memory of the peasants of El Salvador.

During the long dictatorship of General Martinez (1932-45), the first of a series of military regimes which have ruled the country ever since, the activities of the labour movement were severely curtailed and the economy continued to be controlled by the '14 families' of the oligarchy. In 1945 President Castaneda Castro authorised the establishment of the Centre for Trade Union Unification (CUS), and Colonel Osorio, who took over in 1948, formally extended recognition to urban unions although rural organisations were still banned. Many new unions were formed in the 1950s. The most powerful of these was the Federation of Railway Workers which negotiated a collective contract with the railway companies after a successful strike.

The labour movement at this time was dominated by ORIT and the Communist Party was forced to work underground, especially during the government of Jose Maria Lemus (1956-60). The General Confederation of Trade Unions (CGS) was established in 1958 and to remain close to the government for the next two decades. In October 1979 the CGS was expelled from the ICFTU because of its blatant collaboration with the dictatorship of General Romero (1977-79).

Under President Rivera (1962-67) El Salvador moved towards the creation of a formal democratic political structure. The US Alliance For Progress aid programme and the formation of the Central American Common Market (CACM) encouraged economic development and a degree of industrialisation. However, the 1963 labour code was designed to keep the working class firmly in check. Unions were to be dissolved if they called or encouraged sympathy strikes or engaged in 'subversive activities'.

Labour unrest increased in the mid-1960s as workers gained in self-confidence and the working class stengthened under the effects of the CACM. The independent unions, representing about 25% of the organised labour force, took up particularly radical positions while the church founded the Federation of Catholic Trade Unions and the Union of Catholic Workers which both organised small peasant leagues in the countryside. A strike by steelworkers at a Japanese-owned factory in 1967 was supported by a series of sympathy strikes and resulted in a victory for the workers. The military was caught off guard by this militancy and solidarity and the long teachers strike in 1968 was subjected to fierce repression as a result. Nevertheless, the working class was moving ahead as a whole and this, combined with the growth of small but voluble christian and social democratic

Mass organisations demonstrate in San Salvador—1979. CALA

parties and the emergence of a communist party electoral front, threatened the dominance of the '14 families' which moved to tighten the political and military defence of their monopoly over the economy. In the countryside mounting tension caused by the lack of land was met by the government provoking the so-called 'football war' with Honduras to divert attention from domestic issues.

The political situation continued to deteriorate and the labour and peasant movements came under increasing attacks. The rigged elections of 1972, 1974 and 1976, in which massive fraud prevented the opposition parties from coming to power confirmed

the anti-democratic nature of the military regimes and further polarised the country. As it became more and more obvious that the dominant classes would not surrender power the steady decline of the political parties was mirrored by the rise of the

mass popular organisation which mobilised radical opposition to the army and the oligarchy. The most important of these were the Front for United Popular Action (FAPU) and the Popular Revolutionary Bloc (BPR), founded in 1974 and 1975 respectively. General Carlos Humberto Romero came to power in 1977 through electoral fraud, the pattern of his rule being set when troops killed 20 workers at the May Day demonstration that year. At the end of the year a wave of strikes led the regime to introduce the draconinan Law of Public Order which tightly restricted all union and political activity and effectively held the country under a state of siege. However, the occupation of the ministry of labour by the BPR in the same month forced the regime and employers to make some concessions to striking workers. Repression in the countryside was particularly fierce. In addition to the activities of the armed forces, right wing death squads and the government-controlled paramilitary force ORDEN took a regular toll of victims, leaving their bodies on the road side to intimidate the peasants.

Conflict increased in 1979 as strike action and guerrilla activity challenged the regime. A series of strikes in March indicated the growing strength and unity of the labour movement under the leadership of the popular organisations. A 24-hour strike called by the power workers union (STCEL) in support of stoppages in the La Constancia and La Tropical soft drinks factories as well as their own grievances brought the industry of San Salvador to a complete halt. The STCEL won most of its demands but repression continued. The fight for trade union rights and a decent standard of living had now merged with the struggle to overthrow the

dictatorship and Romero was finally removed in a coup by young officers in October 1979 in an attempt to forestall growing radicalisation.

Several dozen workers were killed in the first few days of the new government when troops were sent into clear out occupied factories and as a response the BPR occupied the ministries of labour and economy, presenting the new junta with a list of demands. These included compensation for all laid-off factory workers, 100% wage increases for agricultural workers in the harvest season, lower prices for food and consumer goods, free water, settlement of all outstanding labour disputes, freedom for political prisoners, indemnity payments to families of the victims of repression and the immediate dissolution of ORDEN.

While some wage rises were granted and the prices of selected goods frozen, the agrarian and other seemingly major reforms proposed by the junta were never implemented. ORDEN was not disbanded — it simply changed its name — and neither was the repression halted, instead it increased. By the end of 1979 it was clear that the junta offered nothing but continued oppression for the workers and peasants and the bulk of the civilian politicans quit the government, leaving only some of the Christian Democrats to support the young officers, who were by now totally reliant on US backing. The level of repression has risen well above that which existed under Romero: in the first three months of 1980 2,000 people died in the political violence. As the right wing groups build up their campaign against the mass organisations it is plain that El Salvador is on the verge of a civil war.

The working class is at the forefront of this struggle and in the Spring of 1980 the mass organisations launched two political general strikes against the government and the right wing. The first, on 17 March, received near total support in San Salvador and 80% backing in the rest of the country. At least 120 workers were killed on 17 March alone by the military and the right wing terror squads. The second, week-long, strike, was declared after Archbishop Oscar Arnulfo Romero, the progressive Bishop of San Salvador, was killed by rightists. This assassination was clearly intended to provoke an uprising by the forces of the left which could then be wiped out by the army but the popular organisations, well aware of their military weaknesses and the vulnerability of the labour movement, maintained discipline and continued with their strategy of building mass support in both town and countryside for the bitter struggle that lies ahead.

Power workers strike against the government, 1979.

GUATEMALA

POPULATION	6.1 million
ECON. ACTIVE	1.9 million
UNIONISED	6% (ALAI)
UNEMPLOYED	45% (University of San Carlos, Guatemala)
LIFE EXPECTANCY	57.8 years

CONFEDERATIONS

CNT — Confederacion Nacional de Trabajadores (1968). Independent, previously affiliated to CLAT. Claimed 17,000 members in 1978. Apartado 2472, Guatemala City.

CTF — Confederacion de Trabajadores Federados (1970). Affil. ORIT. Claims 50,000. Supports government.

FASGUA — Federacion Autonoma Sindical de Guatemala (1955). Affil. CPUSTAL.

FTG — Federacion de Trabajadores de Guatemala. Independent. Claims 8,000 (Oct. 1979).

CNUS — Consejo Nacional de Unidad Sindical (1976). Established by CNT and FASGUA. Apartado 2472, Guatemala City. Most important members include:

    CUC — Comite de Unidad Campesina (1978) (peasants)

    FENOT — Federacion Nacional de Obreros del Transporte

    FNM — Frente Nacional Magisterial (teachers)

    SCTM — Sindicato Central de Trabajadores Municipales (municipal workers)

    SIMCOS — Sindicato de Trabajajores de los Medios de Comunicacion Social (communications workers)

    CETE — Consejo de Entidades de Trabajadores del Estado (state employees). Illegal.

    Asociacion de Periodistas de Guatemala (journalists)

    AEU — Asociacion de Estudiantes Universitarios (students)

Mutualist societies and craft unions first made their appearance in Guatemala towards the end of the last century. Many of them joined the country's first important federation, the Labour Federation of Guatemala for the Protection of Work, established in 1914. The labour movement made some advances in organisation and working conditions but suffered a great deal of repression under the dictatorship of Manuel Estrada Cabrera (1900-21). The first major strikes involved railway and telegraph workers in 1920. The rail workers won a wage increase but they were not so successful in 1924 when the government intevened and imprisoned labour leaders. In the same year, government troops broke a month long strike by United Fruit Company dock workers, and many were killed, arrested or expelled from the country. In 1926, the Regional Federation of Guatemalan Workers was formed by 13 unions with more than 2,000 members.

During the dictatorship of Jorge Ubico (1931-44) trade unions were banned and the few gains the labour movement had made were cancelled. New legislation strongly favoured employers: for example, a 1934 vagrancy law forced rural workers 'without fixed employment' to provide labour on agricultural estates.

During the decade 1944-54, the labour movement made significant advances under the democratic reformist governments of Presidents Juan Jose Arevalo and Jacobo Arbenz. The 1947 labour code was a comprehensive document protecting the workers' right to organise and establishing minimum wages, social security and the eight hour day among other benefits. Such clauses as the stipulation that union officials could not be dismissed by a company during their term of office or for six months after its expiry indicate the tone of the labour code and the government's attitude to labour relations. A system of labour courts and inspectorates was established to ensure that the new labour code was complied with. The Confederation of Guatemalan Workers (CTG), established in 1944, was able to claim over 500 affiliates and 104,000 members by 1954.

A group of peasants receiving land in 1953.

The removal of restrictions on rural unions and the creation of the National Confederation of Guatemalan Peasants (CNCG) in 1950 was followed by a wave of peasant organisation. By 1954, the CNCG was said to have 1,700 affiliates with a quarter of a million members. The progressive nature of the government, the threat posed to landed wealth by rural mobilisation, the direct threat to US economic interests, and the possibility of the Guatemalan 'revolution' spreading to other Central American countries, prompted a CIA backed coup which overthrew Arbenz and brought Castillo Armas to power in 1954.

Since that date, workers and peasants have continually had to struggle to maintain auth-

Colonel Carlos Castillo Armas.

After the earthquake of 1976.

entic trade unions. Physical repression, blacklisting, divisionism and corruption have kept the labour movement on the defensive for nearly three decades. The only unions that have been able to organise freely have been those linked to ORIT. The army's determination to stamp out guerilla activity that emerged in the early 1960s in response to the impossibility of achieving change through democratic means, plunged the country into a long period of violence in which not only the guerillas but also labour and peasant leaders and organisations were a target for the security forces.

The situation deteriorated under the civilian government of Mendez Montenegro (1966-70) and violence was institutionalised under the presidency of Colonel Arana Osorio (1970-74) who had led the counter-insurgency campaign against the guerillas in the late 1960s. Arana's first act was to declare a state of siege which paralysed union activities and his presidency was marked by a sharp increase in political violence in which right-wing terrorist groups condoned by the government were responsible for over 15,000 deaths, mainly trade unionists and peasants.

General Kjell Laugerud (1974-78) promised to restore trade union rights but, following the destruction and dislocation of economic activity caused by the 1976 earthquake, tension increased as trade unions tried to organise more effectively to fight for their basic rights and against repression by the state and victimisation by employers. In March 1976, an important step towards labour unity was taken with the creation of the National Council for Trade

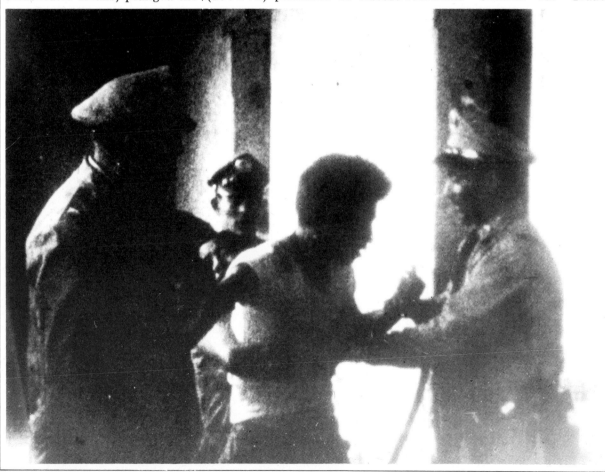

Union Unity (CNUS). The government's response to the increasing combativity of the labour movement was a further increase in repression. The assassination of Lopez Larrave, legal advisor to CNUS and a key figure in the labour movement, was a severe blow but only one of the tens of murders committed each month by the right-wing death squads created by the government, employers and landowners.

Despite the intimidation, CNUS continued to grow in strength and authority and workers openly demonstrated their opposition to the regime. Indicative of the spirit of many workers at this time was the protest march undertaken by 300 miners from their homes in Ixtahaucan to Guatemala City in November 1977 in response to the announced closure of mines and company attempts to destroy the miners' union. After an eight day march of 160 miles the miners were welcomed in the capital by at least 60,000 people in a huge demonstration of working class solidarity. The authorities were forced to back down in the face of such a powerful and well-disciplined mobilisation, although they later cut the workforce at the mines and Mario Mujia of the CNT, a leading organiser of the march, was subsequently assassinated.

Meanwhile, the massacre by troops and landowners of over 100 peasants in the northern village of Panzos in May 1978 indicated the level of tension and repression in the countryside. The discovery of natural resources, including nickel and oil, the construction of a transcountry pipeline, and the associated penetration of multinational companies in the area, has increased the value of the land and the pressure on the peasantry.

The unions' increased strength resulted in several minor victories for workers in 1978 culminating in the general strike of 2 October when the doubling of public transport fares in the capital triggered a week of demonstrations and barricades in the streets. It was only after 30 people had died and over 100 had been injured that the government revoked the fare increase. However, the repression continued. Army and police units forcibly removed protesters occupying key buildings, assassination attempts were made on Israel Marquez, general secretary of the CNT and leader of the Coca Cola union, and Marco Hernandez, leader of the CETE (public sector workers). On 18 October, the Secret Anti-Communist Army (ESA), a right-wing death squad, published a list of 38 people it condemned to death, including many trade union leaders. On 21 October, Oliverio Castaneda de Leon, president of the students' union, was assassinated in full view of hundreds of people; two days later, the CETE and two of the oldest and most combative unions, the postmen and telecommunications workers, were declared illegal. The momentum of this offensive did not slacken: the right-wing paramilitary groups continued their campaign of assassinations while official forces of the regime raided factories and enforced sacking following the October strike. The effect of this was to instil a climate of fear and insecurity both in the towns and the countryside.

Nevertheless, 50,000 workers marched through the capital city on May Day 1979 under the eyes of the police and more sinister spectators — armed men in civilian clothes in cars with no number plates — trade marks of the death squads. Meanwhile, in May, President Lucas Garcia (1978-) and 100 businessmen and government officials attended a conference sponsored by the International Trade Mart of New Orleans at which they extolled the virtues of Guatemala. A pamphlet handed out at the conference spoke of the favourable labour legislation in Guatemala and the 'wonderful relations between labour and capital'. The government has prepared a new labour code which will doubtless contribute to this happy state of affairs. The labour code, presented at the end of 1979, was roundly rejected by CNUS for its contravention of ILO conventions on labour freedoms and open support for the interests of capital. CNUS was also instrumental in establishing the Democratic Front Against Repression (FDCR), in February 1979, which brings together over 150 unions, 160 peasant organisations and other groups in a national political front opposed to the government.

In February 1980, the regime was forced into a partial but significant retreat by the all-out strike of 50,000 sugar workers on the Pacific coast at the height of the harvest. The workers demanded an increase in pay from US$1.12 to $5.00 a day. After a fortnight the government decreed an increase to US$3.20 which was vehemently opposed by the employers. The success of the strike revealed that there exists a remarkable potential for mobilisation and organisation amongst the workers and peasants of Guatemala.

However, this is constantly threatened by the intense repression — by June 1980 an average of 20 were being murdered every day. Attacks on trade unionists have reached such a point that on Saturday June 21 the regime, in a clear attempt to eradicate the leadership of the working class, raided the CNT headquarters and abducted the entire 27-strong executive committee who disappeared without trace.

GUYANA

POPULATION	800,000
ECON. ACTIVE	250,000
UNIONISED	
UNEMPLOYED	33% (UGSA)
LIFE EXPECTANCY	69.1 years

UNIONS

TUC — Trades Union Congress. 27 unions. Supports government.

CCWU — Clerical and Commercial Workers Union.

GAWU — General Agricultural Workers Union. 20,000 (Includes sugar workers).

GLU — Guyana Labour Union (waterfront workers).

GMWU — Guyana Mine Workers Union (bauxite miners).

NAACIE — National Association of Agricultural, Clerical and Industrial Employees.

UGSA — University of Guyana Staff Association.

Slaves from Africa and indentured labour from Asia were brought by the British to provide a workforce for the sugar plantation-based economy in what was their only colony on the South American mainland. The last 40 years have seen the development of a militant trade union movement that is currently facing a strong attack from the government led by Forbes Burnham of the Peoples' National Congress (PNC).

The first unions were formed in the 1920s when Hubert Critchlow, regarded as the father of trade unionism in Guyana, founded the British Guiana Labour Union (BGLU) in 1922. The following years saw industrial action involving sugar, waterfront, railway, and factory workers but few substantial advances were made. In the 1930s the slump in the world price for sugar caused by the depression led to a wave of labour unrest throughout the Caribbean. This gave an impetus to union organisation and led to violent clashes with British security forces. In 1939 police opened fire on a demonstration at Leonora and killed four workers.

The focus of labour unrest in British Guiana was the sugar plantation. In 1936 the Man Power Citizens' Association (MPCA) was formed but this organisation soon fell under the influence of the owners who employed a mixture of bribery and intimidation to undermine its effectiveness. Strikes occurred at regular intervals in the 1940s, culminating in a four month-long stoppage on eight estates on the east coast of Demerera under the slogan of 'sit and starve rather than work

and starve'. The response of the colonial administration was repression. On 16 June 1946 police attacked a group of workers on the Enmore plantation, killing five and wounding 12.

These years saw the creation of the Guiana Industrial Workers Union (GIWU) as the spearhead of an increasingly militant working class and a growing political movement for independence from Britain. The 1953 elections arranged by the colonial administration resulted in a victory for the Peoples' Progressive Party (PPP) of Cheddi Jagan who enjoyed strong popular and trade union backing, especially from the Asian and rural workers.

The Jagan government embarked upon a series of reforms, including a labour relations bill which required employers to negotiate with unions enjoying majority support in the workforce. The bill also contained clauses prohibiting the victimisation of workers and giving trade union officials the right to visit places where their members were employed. With a general strike threatening the employers and the presence of a government ready to introduce legislation such as this in defence of the workers the British acted quickly, sending warships and aircraft to the capital, Georgetown, and occupying the country which was still formally under their control. The constitution was suspended and emergency regulations imposed, severely restricting trade union and political activity.

When elections were held again, in 1957, the PPP was once again victorious, although real power was witheld from the government formed by Jagan. Although the following years saw the introduction of some legislation favourable to workers, the British infiltrated the trade union movement very effectively, controlling its growth and stifling militancy.

The early 1960s were violent years with general strikes against the Jagan government in years with general strikes against the Jagan government in 1962 and 1963. There were two major reasons for this turn in events. First, the emergence of Burnham's PNC with support among the predominantly black industrial working class in opposition to the PPP. Second, British and US anxiety at the possibility of a radical government under Jagan leading Guyana to full independence and into the socialist camp in alliance with Cuba. The country's geographical position and its proven reserves of bauxite and other strategic minerals led the United States to finance and organise direct opposition to Jagan, primarily through the CIA and the AIFLD.

Then, in 1964, the British called new elections under a new proportional representation scheme that effectively prevented the PPP from winning an outright majority. After an indecisive result Burnham's PNC was invited to form a government, and it was to this government that independence was granted in 1966. Although the PNC nationalised key sectors of the economy, its government has become increasingly corrupt and repressive over the years. A series of election frauds beginning in 1973 has led to fears that the PNC intends to eliminate all political opposition in the country.

Government austerity measures and a decline in living standards (over 25% in the last

five years according to the World Bank) led to a sugar plantation strike in 1977 and a major miners strike in 1979. When the plantation workers struck in 1977 it was in support of the demand for a full share of the industry's profits for the period 1974-76 (when international prices for sugar soared). However, the regime refused to make any concessions and used scab labour to break the strike. The Trinidad and Tobago Oil Workers Union refused to handle petrol destined for Guyana in solidarity but police harassment and the GAWU's lack of finance forced the workers back to work. This was a substantial defeat but it took place in a period of increasing militancy, one of the products of which was the emergence of the Working Peoples' Alliance (WPA), formally constituted as a party in July 1979. The WPA which, despite its cooperation with the PPP, appeals to workers of both major ethnic groups in Guyana has now become a major political force. It receives much support from the miners but has also concentrated on organising the peasants and rural workers, and the sympathy for the WPA's radical politics amongst broad sectors of workers has been one of Burnham's principal concerns in the recent period.

The biggest confrontation in the last few years was the strike of the bauxite miners in 1979 after the state mining company violated an agreement over increments during training periods. The dispute then turned into a struggle over wages, lasting six weeks and rapidly developing into a general protest against economic mismanagement and political repression. The GAWU, NAACIE, CCWU and UGSA, the most progressive unions, all came out in sympathy with the miners. The government refused to give any

ground and pursued its usual course of action. Police harassment of strikers and picket lines, confiscation of food intended for the miners, the short-term imprisonment of union leaders and a massive anti-strike campaign in the officially-controlled media all placed considerable pressure on the workers.

Burns Bonadie, secretary of the Caribbean Congress of Labour (CLL), visited Guyana to see the situation for himself and strongly condemned the regime's activities. 'The entire Caribbean trade union movement' he said 'is looking on at what is happening in Guyana. When the trade union movement is being done away with, it is clear that the stage is being set for dictatorship'. The strike ended with the main issue going to arbitration and the GMWU leadership bowing to pressure from the regime. This widened the gap between the leadership and the rank and file who had to force official recognition of the strike in the first place. Although the GMWU was originally an important power base for the PNC with its predominantly black membership, this is no longer the case as the bulk of the miners have moved to more radical positions. The WPA is now banned from holding meetings in the Linden mining camp where increasingly repressive rules have been introduced, one of which gives supervisors the authority to suspend workers suspected of dis discussing politics.

With Burnham apparently intent upon holding on to power by whatever means necessary, one of which is most certainly the strict containment of the working class and small farmers, it is clear that the labour movement in Guyana will have to embark upon a major political as well as economic struggle in order to defend its interests.

HAITI

POPULATION	4.6 million
ECON. ACTIVE	2.8 million
UNIONISED	
UNEMPLOYED	70% (including underemployment)
LIFE EXPECTANCY	52.2 years

The first important labour organisation in Haiti was the Worker Federation of Haiti which devoted most of its energies to opposing the occupation of the country by United States marines (1915-34). Stenio Vincent (1930s) and Elie Lescot (1941-46) ruled the country with an iron hand giving little opportunity for the organisation of a labour movement. The government of President Dumarsais Estime (1946-50) was the first to allow trade unions to organise. The Federation of Haitian Workers (FTH) was founded in 1946 and claimed the affiliation of 51 unions. A split in this organisation occurred in 1948 with the formation of the Haitian Federation of Labour (FHT) which criticised communist influence in the FTH and affiliated itself to ORIT. By 1949 it was the strongest organisation with its greatest following among the port, transport and manufacturing workers of the capital, Port-au-Prince. Also established at this time was the National Union of Workers (UNT) under the leadership of Daniel Fignole. This organised sugar, white collar and some industrial workers.

In 1948, there were 153 unions in the country with 53% of these in the capital. Under Estime's government, a ministry of labour was established and the foundations of a rudimentary social security system were laid. In 1949, the FHT split with a small group emerging called the Trade Union Federation of Haiti which became the General Confederation of Labour in 1950. The dictatorship of Paul Magloire (1950-56) put a brake on this activity, although the FHT tried to unify the trade unions in the National

Union of Labour (aff. ORIT). Magloire fell in 1956 and the following year 'Papa Doc' Duvalier came to power. The Intersindical Union of Haiti (1958) and the Federation of Christian Trade Unions managed to retain a degree of independence but they were unable to survive long under the reign of terror conducted by the Duvalier regime. Although unions continued to exist, all officials were in the pay of employers or the government and strikes were outlawed.

This fierce opposition and the very low level of industrialisation meant that there was virtually no trade union activity for nearly 20 years. Papa Doc died in 1971 and was succeeded by his son Jean Claude who at first tried to promote a less repressive image. The last three years have seen major developments in the Haitian labour movement. In May 1976, the first strike for many years in the cement industry was violently repressed. The strike leaders and workers were not the only ones to suffer. The journalist Gasner Raymond of *Le Petit Samedi Soir* was assassinated for reporting on the strike. Sugarmill, cement and some mining company unions (e.g. Reynolds) have emerged as combative organisations. Their primary demand is the right to independent unions with leaders elected by the workers instead of chosen by the employer. The very fact that workers have begun to take action at all is a development of great importance in Haiti. In 1977, peasants demonstrated in front of the National Palace and workers at the United States owned Hasco sugar mill went on strike. These two groups of workers repeated their action in 1978. The Hasco strikers demanded an 80% wage rise and the right to elect their own officials. Such demands have not been met but cement workers recently received a 16% wage rise after industrial action.

Haiti is the poorest country in the western hemisphere although the Duvalier family fortune is estimated to be several hundred million dollars. 10,000 to 15,000 workers are 'sold' each year to the Dominican Republic for work on the sugar estates just over the border. These workers receive the barest minimum wage, but the 70% unemployment in Haiti means that they must take the work or face death by starvation. Although there are plenty of unemployed Dominicans, the estate owners prefer to employ the more easily exploitable Haitians. The Duvalier regime takes a fee for each worker exported for the harvest season. In 1979, a total of 1.4 million dollars was handed over to the Haitian government for the services of these 'braceros' (80 dollars per head).

United States companies seeking ever cheaper labour supply in the Caribbean are coming to Haiti in greater numbers. Those groups of workers who challenge employers are still in an extremely weak position and although the recent development of light industry has increased the industrial workforce the great majority of Haiti workers remain landless rural labourers lacking any organisation or protection from the extraordinary level of exploitation to which they are subjected. As a consequence there are still no formally constituted federations in the country and labour organisation is limited to rank and file actions at plant level.

'Baby Doc', suitably armed. The Duvalier family fortune is an estimated 200 million dollars, GNP per capita 200 dollars a year.

HONDURAS

POPULATION	3.3 million
ECON. ACTIVE	1.0 million
UNIONISED	
UNEMPLOYED	10%
LIFE EXPECTANCY	52.1 years

CONFEDERATIONS

CGT — Confederacion General de Trabajadores (1969) Affil. CLAT. Includes: FASH — Federacion Autentica Sindical de Honduras (1963); Federacion de Sindicatos de Trabajadores de la Banca-Financiera (bank workers); Federacion Hondurena de Sindicatos de Trabajadores de la Alimentacion (food workers); Federacion Nacional de Pobladores (shantytown dwellers); FESISUR — Federacion Sindical del Sur (southern regional federation); UNC — Union Nacional de Campesinos (peasants); STINCAH (construction workers); SITIAMA (metal workers); SITIAMASH (food and drink workers).

CTH — Confederacion de Trabajadores de Honduras (1964) Affil. ORIT. Includes: FESINTRAH — Federacion de Sindicatos de Traba-jadores del Norte de Honduras (1957) 42 unions with 27,000 members. Amongst the most important of these are SITRACIAG — Sindicato de Trabajadores del Campo, Industrias Agricolas y Ganaderias (rural workers) 7,500; SOEM — Sindicato de Obreros Mineros de el Mochito (miners 1,500; SITRACEHSA — Sindicato de Trabajadores de Cementos de Honduras (cement workers); SUTRAFSCO — Sindicato de Trabajadores de Standard Fruit Company, 7,000. ANACH — Asociacion Nacional de Campesinos de Honduras (1963) (peasants).

Comite Intersindical (1977) Inter-Union Committee. Based in the industrial north, especially around San Pedro Sula. 40 affiliates. In 1978 16 of these affiliates were CGT unions. Includes SITIAMASH; STINCAH; UNC and UNCAH — Union Nacional de Campesinos Autenticos de Honduras (peasants).

FUNACAMH — Frente de Unidad Nacional Campesino de Honduras (1979). United front of peasant unions. Includes UNCAH and UNC, and has the unofficial support of the majority of ANACH. 100,000.

The Honduran labour movement is the youngest in Latin America. The first strikes took place in the 1920s and 1930s but it was not until 1954 that the unions, influenced by the gains made by workers in neighbouring Guatemala since 1945, began to make significant advances. The turning point came when the United Fruit Company (UFC) workers on the north coast went on strike for better conditions and increased wages in April 1954. Although the local labour court ruled against the strike, it spread to all the northern ports and cut communications with the capital, Tegucigalpa. Radio broadcasts from Guatemala encouraged the workers to stand firm in their demand for a 50% pay rise. By May 50,000 workers were on strike and all the major multinationals were paralysed. President Galvez sent troops to the north but the dispute was ended after mediation by trade unionists from the US and ORIT. Some strike leaders were jailed and increased efforts were made to divide the workers but the major demands were conceded.

One of the causes of this success was the solidarity of the peasants who fed the strikers and their families. After the strike the major fruit companies increased mechanisation which halved their labour force over the next ten years. The first to be fired were union militants who, on rejoining the peasantry, began to organise in the countryside and played a leading role in the development of a large and powerful peasant movement by the late 1960s.

A further result of the strike was the recognition of the Tela

Railroad Workers Union (SITRATERCO) and the Standard Fruit Company Workers Union (SUTRASFCO). The labour code issued in 1959 under President Ramon Morales encouraged unionisation but also enabled employers to evade their new responsibilities. For example, UFC rented its land out to Hondurans who would employ less than 30 peasants and thus avoid the possibility that the local union would receive legal recognition. After pressure from SITRATERCO the regime prohibited such abuses. Meanwhile, ORIT representatives used their influence and money to establish a firm grip on the Honduran trade unions. Nevertheless, many strikes took place in the 1960s, culminating in the 1968 general strike against economic measures introduced following the formation of the Central American Common Market. On this occasion the government declared a state of siege. The peasant organisations suffered most heavily in the 1960s, and after the 1963 military coup repression led to many deaths and the arrest of hundreds of peasants.

In the early 1970s more moderate elements held sway in the government but the timid agricultural reforms proposed by President Lopez Arellano could not overcome determined opposition by the large landowners. The next few years saw a rapid deterioration in the position of the labour movement as successive military governments maintained repression. The presidency of Colonel Melgar Castro (1975-78) saw a sharp turn to the right, a process that was intensified when a military triumvirate came to power in August 1978. Since then repression has continued to increase although workers have occasionally been able to defend their position and force through small gains.

The Management . . . and . . .   Cornell Capa

the banana workers in Honduras. CALA

The unions in the north of the country have been particularly hard hit over the last three years. The placing of the Texaco workers under military discipline, the takeover of SUTRASFCO by company stooges, and the smashing of the Las Isletas agricultural cooperative clearly indicated the direction of government policy. The Las Isletas cooperative had been set up by Standard Fruit workers on abandoned company land. Its success was an alarm signal for Standard Fruit who collaborated with the local army commander to remove the cooperative's leadership and substitute more pliable officials.

A series of isolated disputes took place during 1978 with strikes being followed by company attempts to set up parallel unions. Intimidation, victimisation, bribery and blacklisting are all regularly used with varying success by Honduran employers. The most controversial dispute to occur in 1979 took place at the Bemis Handel textile factory in San Pedro Sula. When the workers occupied the factory after a long dispute over working conditions paramilitary police units stormed the building and killed three workers. The factory was burnt to the ground and the workers accused of arson by the government and the management. However, since the regime has released those accused of the crime and dropped all charges, suspicions that the company set fire to the plant as a way of avoiding the costs of bankruptcy seem to be borne out. Among the points at issue in the dispute was the workers' refusal to accept the installation of closed circuit television throughout the factory for use in monitoring their activities. Both during and after the occupation local employers filled the press with advertisements demanding that the government teach the unions a harsh lesson. With tension rising steadily, especially in the north and the countryside, a major clash seems inevitable before long.

The radicalisation of many unions and the decreasing influence of ORIT affiliates has led to the formation of more militant union alliances including the Inter-Union Committee. This committee contains dissident ORIT-affiliated unions, which have come under the influence of the CP, and the General Confederation of Workers (CGT). The CGT remains affiliated to CLAT although its relationship with the headquarters in Caracas has been far from easy. In 1978 CLAT demanded control of the CGT's external finance, and when the CGT refused a split looked likely but eventually the issue was resolved with the Hondurans retaining control over funds from abroad. The Inter-Union Committee's real strength comes from the peasant organisations, particularly UNCAH and UNC (both effectively controlled by the CGT) and the progressive wing of ANACH which has the support of the majority of the members but has been refused recognition by the government. In all there are some 100,000 members in this peasant front.

Although Honduras has yet to feel the full impact of the rising political conflict in Central America, there can be little doubt that developments in Guatemala as well as El Salvador and Nicaragua will encourage Honduran workers and peasants to develop their organisation and fight the repression of the military regime.

JAMAICA

POPULATION	2.1 million
ECON. ACTIVE	900,000
UNIONISED	
UNEMPLOYED	24.5% (1978)
LIFE EXPECTANCY	70.6 years

UNIONS

BITU — Bustamente Industrial Trade Union (1939). Linked to Jamaican Labour Party. 100,000.

NWU — National Workers Union (1952). Linked to Peoples National Party. 100,000. 130, East Street, Kingston. (Tel: 922 1150 or 6692)

CS — Congreso Sindical. Linked to PNP. 12,000.

JALGO (municipal employees). 10,000.

UWA — United Workers Alliance.

Civil Service Association.

Teachers Association.

Although labour unrest was commonplace in the first decades of the century, it was not until the end of the Second World War that significant industrial action took place and lasting unions were formed. The Jamaican Federation of Labour was formed in 1918 and during the next two years railway workers, teachers and civil servants went on strike, which resulted in several deaths. Railway workers won their demands but their organisation was undermined by the posting of their leaders to workshops away from the capital. Another attempt to organise a trade union movement occurred in 1929/30 with the establishment of the Jamaica Trades and Labour Union, but it did not survive very long.

A turning point came in 1938 when rioting workers

'I'd rather be a free man in my grave Than live as a puppet or a slave . . .'　Ron Smith

throughout the island demonstrated their opposition to the British colonial government and poor working conditions and wages. The following years saw the emergence of the nationalist movement in which the labour movement played a prominent role. Trade union leaders Alex Bustamente and Norman Manley later became leading political figures and led the country to independence in 1962.

The Jamaican Labour Party (JLP) was in office for the next ten years, but the People's National Party (PNP) led by Michael Manley won the elections in 1972, with popular support for its commitment to introduce major economic and social reforms. The JLP, on the other hand, is known to have collaborated with the CIA in attempts to 'destabilise' Jamaica after the pattern of Chile.

In the late 1970s, the PNP's attempts to carry out their programme of structural reforms was severely hampered by world economic trends, natural disasters and a steep decline in sugar prices. Despite these economic difficulties and

the destabilisation campaign of the opposition, the PNP was returned to power in 1976 with an increased majority. However, social unrest has risen, reaching a climax in 1979 with strikes in many sectors. Manley was forced to turn to the International Monetary Fund (IMF) to help the country out of its economic difficulties and this meant a brake on wage rises, major cuts in government spending and severe hardship for workers.

In early 1980, the economic crisis and the failure to fulfil IMF conditions obliged Manley to break with the IMF and call a general election. Although the government has accepted the necessity of renegotiating its loans with the private banks, the eventual outcome of this episode may be to deepen the island's ties with Cuba. But, whatever the longer term prospects may be, it is clear that the working class is facing severe economic difficulties and in the present climate of acute political tension it will have to continue mobilisation to defend its political rights and advance its economic position.

MEXICO

POPULATION	69.4 million
ECON. ACTIVE	19.7 million
UNIONISED	24%
UNEMPLOYED	45% (including underemployed – LANL)
LIFE EXPECTANCY	64.0 years

CONFEDERATIONS

CGT – Confederacion General de Trabajadores (1921). 34 unions in eight federations with 22,000 members including construction, textile, bakery workers and bus drivers. 5 de Febrero No 73, Mexico DF.

CROC – Confederacion Revolucionaria de Obreros y Campesinos (1952). 254 unions and 140,000 members. Strong in textile, food, hospital and transport unions. San Juan de Letran, No 80-603, Mexico DF.

CROM – Confederacion Regional de Obreros Mexicanos (1918). 193 unions and 150,000 members. Strong in textile, shoe and clothing industries. Concentrated in Puebla, Vera Cruz, Baja California and ports. Republica de Cuba 60, Mexico DF.

CTM – Confederacion de Trabajadores Mexicanos (1936). Affil. ORIT. Vallarta 8, Mexico DF. 10,000 unions with two million members. Includes:
    CNC – Confederacion Nacional de Campesinos (peasants);
    STITRM (textile workers);
    STMMSRM (miners and metal workers);
    STPRM (oil workers);
    SUTERM (electricity workers).

FSTSE – Federacion de Sindicatos de Trabajadores del Estado (1936). Affil. ORIT. 29 national unions with 416,000 members employed by the state. Antonio Caso 35, Mexico DF.

All the above confederations are represented on the Congreso de Trabajo.

INDEPENDENTS

FAT – Frente Autentico de Trabajadores (1960). Affil. CLAT. 53 unions with 50,000 members. Strong in motor industry, especially the Renault and Volkswagen plants.

FNSI – Federacion Nacional de Sindicatos Independientes. 145,000. Monterrey union under control of employers.

UGOCM – Union General de Obreros y Campesinos Mexicanos (1949). Affil. CPUSTAL.

STRM (telephonists); STFRM (railwaymen); SME (electricity workers).

The development of the Mexican labour movement gained impetus in the 1860s and 1870s with the creation of many mutualist societies, the publication of labour journals, and the establishment of the Grand Circle of Workers (1870) and the Grand Confederation of Mexican Worker Associations (1876). These labour organisations declared their non-political nature and sought protective labour laws for the working class. However, a civil code of 1872 forbade strikes and 'worker conspiracies', and the long dictatorship of Porfirio Diaz (1876-1910) brutally repressed the many strikes that took place. During the Revolution (1910-20) the House of

The Mexican Revolution—workers' batallions took part in the fighting.

World Workers organised the urban workers into the so-called 'Red Battalions', which fought for Carranza, one of the several leading protagonists of this long and bloody civil war. Labour organisations were established throughout the area under his control but these were strictly controlled which effectively forestalled any worker-peasant alliance. Carranza later adopted an openly conservative position and was overthrown by another *caudillo*, Obregon, in alliance with organised labour. Labour's role in these years was reflected in the Constitution of 1917 which enshrined workers' rights in article 123.

The Regional Confederation of Mexican Workers (CROM) was established in 1918. CROM worked closely with the government over the next decade. Luis Morones, its leader, entered the cabinet as minister of labour while other leaders became state governors or entered the National Assembly. Labour was therefore afforded some protection and influence, but its leaders inevitably became cut off from ordinary workers. Increasingly bureaucratic and corrupt, CROM steadily lost influence with workers and virtually collapsed when it fell from government favour. Most labour unrest at this time centred around the anarcho-syndicalist General Confederation of Workers (CGT).

The labour movement divided into competing factions and workers made few gains until the presidency of Cardenas (1934-40) who nationalised the oil industry, gave a new impetus to agrarian reform, and encouraged the creation of a new central labour organisation. This body, the Confederation of Mexican Workers (CTM) became the official labour wing of the ruling Institutional Revolutionary Party (PRI). Under Cardenas, the proportion of strikes won by workers increased dramatically and the number of unions rose from 2,000 to 5,000.

The Second World War was a time of relative industrial peace as labour organisations answered the government's appeal for an increase in national production. At the end of the war, the CTM purged radical elements and identified itself very closely with the government. This alliance greatly contributed to the political stability and relatively peaceful labour relations of post-war Mexico. In return for its close control of the labour movement, the CTM has been able to rely on the government to force moderate wage increases and improvements in working conditions from employers. This convenient arrangement has resulted in the CTM bureaucracy and its leader Fidel Velasquez undercutting the collective bargaining role of individual unions and federations, stifling union democracy, and keeping wages below the level many companies could afford to pay. One study has

16% of Mexican workers are employed by foreign companies.

The company, government and union bureaucrats conspire to break an important strike at General Electric in 1974. Excelsior

shown that there was an increase of 180% in the net profits of foreign companies between 1970 and 1974. Any workers or unions that have stepped out of line have had to face a powerful alliance of government, employers and CTM. On occasion, the CTM has adopted a more independent stance in response to unrest among its rank and file and it threatened a general strike in 1974. Strikes by railway workers, teachers and telephone engineers/operators in the late 1950s and 1962 failed to disturb this monolithic structure and it is only in the last decade that the CTM's dominance and control of the labour movement has been threatened. Many independent unions were formed in the 1970s and so-called *tendencias democratas* (democratic tendencies) have emerged within CTM unions in recent years, notably in the electricity and telephone unions.

President Echeverria (1970-76) sponsored various social security and welfare measures to add to the advanced legislation already in existence. A 1973 law extended the social security system, originally established in 1942, to agricultural workers, although in reality few are included. A national workers' housing fund was established in 1972 and the law requires employers to contribute 5% of their wage bill to this fund. As with other measures, such as the profit sharing introduced in 1962, these innovations mostly covered workers in the official labour organisations. In some cases they serve as another instrument for the CTM closely to control the labour movement.

The 1970s saw increased inflation and unemployment. The CTM has cooperated with the present government's wage restraint policy, but independent unions and the *tendencias democratas* have fought to main-

Mexican electrical workers head a demonstration against pro-government union leaders and United States domination of the economy. Punto Critico

tain workers' living standards and fight against unemployment.

Today, the labour movement is restless and unwilling to rely on the CTM. Rising expectations have been frustrated by inflation and unemployment one result of which has been increasing migration to the USA in search of work. The president of the federal conciliation and arbitration board reported that there were 558 strikes in 1978 — 40% more than in 1977. The CTM apparatus is no longer sufficient to keep control of the labour movement. In 1979 it was reported that police, civil

servants and private companies had collaborated to tap the telephones of unionists prior to the negotiation of collective contracts. The authorities admitted that the information obtained had been useful in breaking the strike of the air-traffic controllers at the beginning of 1979.

The recent discovery of huge oil reserves has fuelled expectations of a better standard of living. Unless workers feel that the new found wealth is being distributed fairly, there is likely to be an upsurge of militancy which will break the chains on the labour movement.

NICARAGUA

POPULATION	2.3 million
ECON. ACTIVE	700,000
UNIONISED	
UNEMPLOYED	45% (estimate – Jan. 1980)
LIFE EXPECTANCY	55.2 years

CONFEDERATIONS

CAUS – Central de Accion y Unificacion Sindical (1979). Formed by the Maoist PCN and attacked by the FSLN for collaborating with the CIA to organise strikes in demand of wage rises that the state cannot meet. Not illegal but leaders are periodically jailed.

CGT-i – Confederaction General de Trabajadores independientes (1963). Affil. CPUSTAL. Legal since July 1979, has not joined the FSLN-backed CST but collaborates with it on the Comision Nacional Inter-Sindical (CNI).

CTN – Central de Trabajadores de Nicaragua (1972). Affil. CLAT. Expresses support for the Government of National Reconstruction (GNR) but criticises the CST as an official, non-independent body. Evidence of declining support.

CST – Central Sandinista de Trabajadores (July 1979). No international affiliation. Formed by the FSLN and supported by the GNR, the largest union body in the country with 343 unions and 108,000 members.

CUS – Confederacion de Unificacion Sindical (1964). Affil. ORIT. Losing large numbers of affiliates to the CST and effectively marginalised since July 1979.

ATC – Asociacion de Trabajadores del Campo (1976) (peasants)

The first mutualist societies appeared at the beginning of the century and trade unions emerged after the First World War. In this early period a small newspaper, *La Revolucion Obrera*, was founded which acted as the mouthpiece of working class aspirations. Its editor became minister of labour but failed in his attempts to promote a labour code in the early 1930s. The first attempt at organisation on a national scale came in 1924 when the Organised Labour of Nicaragua (OON) was formed with 15 regional sections. The first major strikes took place in the 1920s against North American fruit and timber companies.

The United States has constantly intervened in the affairs of Nicaragua and US marines were stationed in the country until 1933 when the National Guard was formed under the leadership of Anastasio Somoza. General Sandino, who was to inspire the guerillas of the Sandinista Front for National Liberation (FSLN), led the resistance to the occupation of the country by the US marines, but was assassinated by Somoza in 1934. The OON, which had spoken out in support of Sandino, lost much of its influence.

In 1936, the year in which Somoza installed himself as

President, the newly formed Confederation of Workers of Managua supported the establishment of several agricultural unions on the plantations of the Pacific coast. In 1937, the Confederation of Nicaraguan Workers (CTN) was formed which by 1940 had some 3,000 members in 18 unions. In an attempt to present a more democratic image, Somoza allowed the establishment of the Confederation of Workers of Nicaragua (CTN) in 1944, led by Vicente Lombardo Toledano. In 1945, a labour code was introduced. However, the development of the Cold War encouraged Somoza to smash the labour movement in a period of intense repression which saw most trade union leaders imprisoned or forced to leave the country. Toledano's CTN was dissolved in 1949.

Government controlled federations, such as the General Confederation of Labour (CGT) and the National Confederation of Democratic Trade Unions (CNSD), now dominated the labour scene, although the Federation of Democratic Workers (FTD) spoke out against the government. At the same time, the communists formed the General Union of Workers (UGT), but only four unions were affiliated to it. Many independent unions sprang up in the 1950s, including the Federation of Nicaraguan Workers and Peasants (FOCN), established in 1955, and the Federation of Nicaraguan United Transport Workers (FTUN), established in 1956. By 1970, the FTUN had 3,000 members.

Repression eased during the late 1950s and early 1960s, and in 1963, minimum wage legislation and an agrarian reform law were introduced. These measures were largely cosmetic and had little effect on the lives of agricultural and urban workers, but they gave the workers a greater opportunity for independent organisation. In 1962, a well attended workers' national congress was held. The following year, the CGT split with nearly half the affiliates leaving to form the Federation of Workers of Managua (FTM). This organisation was immediately declared illegal by the government but maintained an unofficial existence until the end of the Somoza dictatorship. It became known as the CGT-i — the Independent CGT — affiliated to CPUSTAL and the WFTU and provided a focus of opposition to the government and the official trade unions. The general secretary of the pro-government CGT, on the other hand, was the vice minister of labour.

By June 1963, a total of 275 unions were officially registered, but many of these were not active. Membership was concentrated around the capital, Managua; less than 1% of paid rural labour was unionised at this time. However, the 1960s did see greater attempts to organise agricultural workers and land invasions in the province of Chinandega in 1962 promoted the establishment of the Nicaraguan Peasant Confederation (CCN). The Autonomous Trade Union Movement of Nicaragua (MOSAN), whose ac-

tivity was concentrated mainly in the countryside, was also established in 1962, and by the end of the decade it had several thousand members. Few of the rural unions were recognised by the government as the law required a minimum of 42 members in a union, 60% of whom had to be literate. However, this did not prevent 534 delegates attending the first national peasants' congress in 1965 and 600 attended a similar congress the year after.

In 1964, the Nicaraguan Trade Union Council (CSN) was formed uniting the pro-government CGT, FTUN and FOCN. This confederation changed its name to the Confederation of Trade Union Unificiation (CUS) in 1969. It

affiliated to ORIT and the ICFTU and maintained a pro-government attitude.

In 1972, MOSAN became the Workers' Centre of Nicaragua (CNT), affiliated to CLAT and the WCL. Its work among rural workers was conducted through the Peasants' Federation of Nicaragua (FCN). The earthquake which destroyed Managua in 1972 was followed by increased inflation and government attempts to speed up the process of reconstruction through increased exploitation of workers. While the Somoza family (the son of the original dictator was now President) and its associates syphoned off international aid into private bank accounts and indulged in massive land speculation in Managua, a government decree was issued increasing the official working week from 48 to 60 hours, cancelling four out of the nine national public holidays, and asking public employees to donate one month's salary for the purposes of national reconstruction.

In response to these moves by the government, the increase in the cost of living and the misery caused by the earth-

Somoza had controlling interests in virtually all Nicaraguan products—gold, coffee, cattle, timber, cotton etc.

quake, the years 1972-73 witnessed the first period of sustained working class opposition to the government in the history of the Nicaraguan labour movement. The boom in the construction industry meant that building workers had a degree of bargaining power and after a 29 day strike by 6,000 workers they gained exemption from the government provisions regulating working hours. Health service workers gained the same victory. Another union prominent in the labour unrest was the textile workers' union which organised a strike of 8,000 workers in ten factories. However, this wave of unrest posed no serious threat to Somoza who bided his time before embarking on a policy of selective repression. The textile workers' union was destroyed and in 1975 Somoza arrested construction, mining, tobacco, banana and electricity union leaders. A downturn in economic activity created massive unemployment which demoralised the workforce and helped to break the labour movement.

The labour movement made little progress in the mid-1970s, although the first May Day demonstration in ten years was held in 1976. In 1977, opposition to the dictatorship mounted throughout the country and the strength of the FSLN (founded in 1962) grew. The daily fight for trade union rights and higher wages became overshadowed by the nationwide move to bring down Somoza. The movement against the dictator comprised much of the business sector as well as the labour movement and resulted in extended strikes throughout 1978 and 1979. The cost of these work stoppages for the working class was very high, but it stood firm.

In September 1978, the FSLN led an insurrection in the major towns in the north of the country. Only the physical

FSLN troops.

destruction of these towns by the National Guard and the air force allowed Somoza to defeat the uprising. In 1979, the FSLN overthrew Somoza after a six month civil war which cost the lives of 40,000 Nicaraguans. The vast majority of the casualties were caused by the indiscriminate bombing of Somoza's air force. This also caused extensive physical damage necessitating a full-scale reconstruction programme following the victory.

The taking of power by the FSLN, and the establishment of the Government of National Reconstruction (GNR) saw rapid changes in the organisation of the labour movement. In July the FSLN set up the

Sandinista Workers Centre (CST) which recruited heavily from other union bodies and by the end of the year had become the largest confederation with the support of 343 unions with 108,000 members. One of its major sources of strength was the Association of Rural Workers (ATC), established in 1976, which played an important role in the civil war by assuring food supplies in the liberated zones, and is now the principal organ for the implementation of the GNR's agrarian reform.

The CST has continued to grow in 1980 with the adhesion of the dockers and banana and coffee workers; it undoubtedly owes its prestige and power to the backing of the FSLN. The CST appears to have taken members primarily from the CUS and the CTN; the former now plays a very marginal role and the latter, while declaring its support for the GNR, is highly criticial of the CST, claiming that it is an official body, incapable of representing the independent interests of the working class. The CGT-i, which organised armed contingents of its members in the war and had a record of consistent opposition

Calculated destruction of property by Somoza on the eve of defeat.

In July 1979 the FSLN commando members and supporters celebrate their victory in the streets of Managua . . . but they had inherited a country in ashes

to the dictatorship, has not entered the CST but collaborates closely with it on the National Inter-Union Commission (CNI), an umbrella organisation established by the FSLN. A fusion between the CST and the CGT-i is planned whereby a united labour body — Trade Union Unity (US) — will represent the bulk of the workers. As yet this proposal has not been realised.

However, the government's labour policy has met with opposition from the left, and particularly from the Centre for Trade Union Action and Unification (CAUS), sponsored by the maoist PCN. CAUS has organised a series of strikes since the Revolution in demand of wage rises which the GNR says would bankrupt the new state. The FSLN leadership has not outlawed CAUS but accused it of working with the CIA and periodically jailed its leading members along with figures from other small left wing groups.

Political problems of this nature are likely to continue, and the condition of the Nicaraguan workers remains very poor as a result of the devastation caused by the war but, nevertheless, the overthrow of Somoza represents a major advance for the working class and peasantry not only in Nicaragua itself but also in the rest of Latin America.

The two faces of Somoza

PANAMA

POPULATION	1.7 million
ECON. ACTIVE	600,000
UNIONISED	15%
UNEMPLOYED	25% (LANL)
LIFE EXPECTANCY	67.9 years

CONFEDERATIONS

CATI — Central Autentica de Traba-jadores Independientes (1976). In-dependent. Three federations, 19 unions with 2,775 members. Includes FAT — Federacion Autentica de Trabajadores, a radical group that split from CIT, and the important construction union SUNTRACS.

CIT—Central Istmena de Trabaja—dores (1959). Affil. CLAT. Six federations, 25 unions with 4,000 members. Apartado 6308, Via Espana 16, Oficina 5, Altos, Panama 5.

CNTP — Central Nacional de Trabaja-dores (1970). Affil. CPUSTAL. Eight federations, 37 unions with 22,000 members. Includes the important SITRACHILCO — Sindicato de Tra-bajadores de Chiriqui Land Company. Apartado 3253, Panama 3.

CTRP — Confederacion de Trabaja-dores de la Republica de Panama (1956). Affil. ORIT. 12 federations, 62 unions with 22,000 members. Apartado 8929, Panama 5.

CPTT — Central Panamena de Trabajadores del Transporte (1975).

CONATO — Comite Nacional de Coordinacion (1970). Government-backed coordinating committee, in-cludes CTRP, CNTP and CIT.

Panama has been ruled by a self-proclaimed 'reformist' government since 1968, when Omar Torrijos, head of the National Guard, and 'a man of the people', took power in a military coup. Recent economic difficulties have precipitated considerable labour unrest, but the country has also been dominated by the negotiations with the United States over the control of the Panama Canal and, therefore, over the country itself.

The existence of the Canal and a high level of immigration from the Caribbean weakened early attempts to organise Pan-ama's workers. The first major national organisation was the Trade Union Federation of Workers of Panama (FSTP), founded in 1930. This united small contingents of transport and office workers and artisans but disappeared in the 1940s.

Although the 1946 Consti-tution recognised trade unions, the 1947 labour code was restrictive and forbade strikes. Legal limitations, the low level of industrialisation and divisions within the labour movement contributed to its weakness. Workers in the Canal Zone were organised by the United Public Workers Union of the United States. The major struggle of the 1950s was the fight of the United Fruit Company workers to form an independent union which was seriously under-mined by the creation of a company union on several occasions. Major strikes in 1960 and 1964 led to violent clashes with the army and the deaths of several workers. The tenacity of the workers forced the company into negotiating a collective contract and recognising the union but another major battle of the 1960s — the typo-graphers' strike of 1965 — ended in defeat and mass sackings. This was also a period of considerable unrest on the sugar plantations where workers staged hunger marches in protest at low wages and poor working conditions.

The populist regime of Tor-rijos, which came to power in 1968, allowed unionisation and collective bargaining and a labour code ratifying this was introduced in 1972. In the period 1969-1977, 131 unions were recognised making a total of 212 unions in the country.

Panamanian students demonstrate against US troops protecting "national" property —the Canal Zone, January 1964.

Panamanian workers demonstrate in solidarity with striking teachers—1979.
Law 95 threatens many gains made by workers in recent years.

However, in 1976, the government introduced Law 95 in response to economic stagnation and a decline in production. This law took away many of the gains made in 1972. A moratorium was placed on all collective contracts, a wage freeze declared, the right to strike curtailed, and lay-offs permitted. The leaderships of the three major confederations agreed to accept the law, but a huge demonstration of 25,000 workers marched on government buildings in protest. It was at this time that the Authentic Independent Workers' Centre (CATI) was formed by unions breaking away from the Isthmian Workers Centre (CIT) in protest at its lack of action. It has been calculated that since 1975 there has been a decline of 5.5% in real wages.

The support of union leaders for Torrijos and the nationalist campaign during the negotiations over the Canal Zone helped to dampen militancy and contain social unrest. Sovereignty over the Canal was formally conceded on 1 October, 1979. Although there had been major strikes of doctors and teachers in 1978, it was only now that the unions broke ranks and began to pursue their members' interests more vigorously. A long strike ended in a major victory for the teachers with large pay rises for primary and secondary school teachers, the scrapping of controversial educational reforms, and the appointment of an official policy commission of eight teachers' representatives and eight government officials under the chairmanship of the education minister.

Major demonstrations against Law 95 took place in November 1979. All the confederations united in claiming that the law had harmed workers' interests without serving to promote investment as expected by the government. The national assembly unanimously approved a workers' resolution that the law be repealed but by the middle of February 1980 the government had still resisted taking any action and the union umbrella organisation CONATO threatened to call an indefinite general strike. The unions' stand on this issue reflects not only the deterioration of the economy but also growing political mobilisation in Central America as a result of the struggles in Nicaragua and El Salvador. This influence promises to break the relative quiescence of Panamanian labour in recent years.

PARAGUAY

POPULATION	2.6 million
ECON. ACTIVE	800,000
UNIONISED	
UNEMPLOYED	6.3% (Asuncion — Banco Paraguayo de Datos)
LIFE EXPECTANCY	61.9 years

CONFEDERATIONS

CNT — Coordinacion Nacional de Trabajadores (1978). Affil. CLAT. Previously known as the Central Nacional de Trabajadores Urbanos (1963). Teniente Farina 2588, Asuncion.

CPT — Confederacion Paraguaya de Trabajadores (1951). Suspended by the ICFTU 1977. The only legal confederation and by far the largest. Yegros 130-133, Asuncion.

CPTE — Confederacion Paraguaya de Trabajadores en el Exilio (1958). Maintains fraternal relations with the ICFTU.

In 1906 the Labour Federation of Paraguay united the 2,000 members of craft unions and societies then existing in the capital, Asuncion. These groups were influenced by the anarcho-syndicalism of Spanish immigrants, one of whom, Rafael Barret, is regarded as the father of the Paraguayan labour movement. In the early years, the port workers were in the vanguard of the struggle for workers' rights. These workers have a strategic role in the Paraguayan economy, as the country, which is the most isolated on the continent, is linked to the outside world by the River Paraguay. Their union, known as the Naval Federation, was established in 1915 and conducted the country's first major strike which lasted nearly two years (1920-21). After the strike the federation split and the moderate Maritime Workers League emerged as the strongest labour group in the country, winning the first important collective contract in 1928. More radical elements formed the nucleus of the Communist Party.

By 1930, radical unions were predominant and formed the National Confederation of Workers (CNT). This was a period of bitter struggles in the tanning factories on the northern banks of the River Paraguay. In 1932, CNT agitation in opposition to the Chaco War with Bolivia caused the government to imprison its leaders and dissolve all labour organisations. As in Bolivia, the end of the Chaco War witnessed the emergence of a radical nationalist government of junior officers. President Franco (1936-37) established a populist regime that incorporated some fascist elements, but many unions were formed in his short period in office. A department of labour was created and legislation established the eight hour working day. The CNT was re-established as the National Confederation of Workers of Paraguay (CNTP).

When Colonel Morinigo took power in 1940, he banned the CNTP and established a puppet organisation called the Republican Workers' Organisation (ORO). After a period of political instability in 1946-47, which resulted in a short civil war, the Colorado Party took power and banned all trade unions apart from ORO, renamed the Paraguayan Confederation of Workers (CPT) in 1951. In the early 1950s independent trade unionists gradually gained control of the CPT under the government of President Chavez, who sympathised with the government of Peron in Argentina. However, in 1954, Chavez was forced out of office by the armed forces shortly before Peron met the same fate. The new President,

General Stroessner, is still in power today, the longest ruling dictator in Latin America. He did not at first attempt to dismantle the trade union organisations, but economic decline and an IMF 'stabilisation plan' led to a severe drop in living standards and a general strike in 1958. Police arrested 300 union leaders and the government dissolved the CPT. Although a reserve leadership took over the organisation of the strike, the unions were effectively crushed. The CPT is still in existence but it is subservient to the dictatorship and is in no way an authentic representative of the labour movement. In 1977, the ICFTU suspended the CPT, whereupon the Confederation promised a more independent line under the new general secretary Dr.

Modesto Ali (his predecessor, Nicanor Fleitas, was the wealthy majority shareholder of an urban bus company). Ali, however, has shown little sign of independence from the regime and pushed for the CPT's disaffiliation from ORIT in 1979.

With the authentic trade unions destroyed and government officials in key posts (a former police chief, Rodolfo Echeverria, became secretary general of the CPT, and a notorious police torturer, Enrique Volta Gaona, became the CPT's legal advisor), there was little breathing space for organised labour. Government control of the trade union bureaucracy, physical repression and the widespread use of police informers combined to suppress the labour movement. Police informers were especially common at the meat packing plant of Zeballos Cue belonging to the British Brooke Bond Liebig company until it closed in 1978.

In the countryside population increase and soil exhaustion led to a decline in living standards. In the 1960s, the Catholic church encouraged the formation of agricultural co-operatives which set up 'agrarian leagues'. This was particularly the case in the provinces of Misiones and Concepcion where there was considerable conflict between small peasants and large landowners. As the leagues became radicalised in the 1970s, the dictatorship stepped in. Thirty priests were expelled from the country and between 1974 and 1976 the police and army destroyed the radical leagues, imprisoned, tortured or killed the leaders, and exiled members to other parts of the country. The leagues have since recovered but are still under intense pressure. In early 1979, Constantino Coronel, one of the national leaders of the movement, narrowly escaped an assassination attempt by the police. He was later arrested in the hospital where he was recuperating from gun shot wounds and is currently in jail on trumped-up charges of subversion, robbery and rape.

After the lean years of 1960-75, the picture has changed under the impact of a major economic boom associated with the construction of the world's largest hydro-electric project at Itaipu Falls on the border with Brazil. This and associated developments have doubled Paraguay's industrial workforce in just five years. The influx of capital has sparked off an inflationary spiral reducing real wages. According to the unions, prices increased 25% between June 1978 and June 1979, but the maximum wage offer made by the government, which assessed inflation to be 6.8%, was 15%. The Itaipu workers are not allowed to organise, but despite their relatively high wages, they pose a threat to the regime. Their concentration in a restricted area, the semi-skilled nature of some of the work and their very real grievances (working conditions and job safety — so far nearly 50 men have died in industrial accidents) could contribute towards unrest.

There has also been renewed activity in the capital where the regime is currently tolerating limited industrial action and where some union leaders are beginning to voice the grievances of their members. However, this action is severely circumscribed. Workers are still to a great extent at the mercy of employers who frequently break contracts and deny workers their rights. The British company Brooke Bond Liebig was at the centre of a recent dispute in which many workers were laid off and denied the appropriate redundancy payments. Among those unions who have recently displayed a greater degree of autonomy and activism are the newly formed Union of Journalists of Paraguay (SPP), whose general secretary was jailed for two months in late 1979 for writing an article on corruption in the government, the National Union of Construction Workers (SINATRAC), the newly formed Union of Business Employees and Workers (SEOC), the Coca Cola Workers Union (SITRAPAR), the National Union of Metallurgical Workers (SINOMA), and the Federation of Bank Workers of Paraguay (FETRABAN).

Stroessner recently celebrated his 25th anniversary in power and the repressive apparatus is intact, but the trade union movement has some room for manoeuvre unlike, for instance, workers in neighbouring Uruguay.

Demonstration by members of the peasant agrarian leagues group against government expropriation of their lands, for the purpose of re-selling at a handsome profit to Brazilians and other foreign buyers such as Brooke Bond Liebig and Gulf & Western.
Andrew Nickson

PERU

POPULATION	15.3 million (1978)
ECON. ACTIVE	5.5 million (1978)
UNIONISED	
UNEMPLOYED	6.5% (1978)
LIFE EXPECTANCY	57.2 years

and metallurgical workers.

CNT — Confederacion Nacional de Trabajadores (1971). Affil. CLAT. Apartado 11,534, Avenida 28 de Julio 569, Lima 11.

CTP — Confederacion de Trabajadores del Peru (1944). Affil. ORIT. Apartado 3626, Lima. 300,000 (1969). Affiliates include sugar, textile, hospital and railway workers' federations. Close to the APRA political party.

CTRP — Confederacion de los Trabajadores de la Revolucion Peruana (1972). Government-backed. Includes oil workers and fishermen's federations.

CCUSC — Comite de Coordinacion y Unificacion de Sindicatos Clasistas (1974).

FNTMMP — Federacion Nacional de Trabajadores Mineros y Metalurgicos del Peru (miners and metal workers). Independent.

SUTEP — Sindicato Unico de Trabajadores Educadores del Peru (teachers). Independent.

At the end of the 19th century groups of artisans formed mutualist societies to regulate competition in their respective trades and give each other economic aid in the event of unemployment or illness. These workers, who were strongly influenced by anarchist ideas, organised congresses in 1896 and 1901. The bakers were prominent in early attempts to organise workers, and in 1905 they invited other sectors to take part in the celebration of international working men's day in Lima. The general strike in Lima in 1911, the formation of the Regional Workers' Federation in 1913, and the creation of the textile workers' union (FTT) in 1919 were all important steps for the Peruvian labour movement. Early struggles centred on winning an 8 hour day, conceded by the government in 1918.

The next decade saw two major developments with the

CONFEDERATIONS

CGTP — Confederacion General de Trabajadores del Peru (1968). Affil. CPUSTAL. The largest confederation. Plaza 2 de Mayo 4, Lima. Affiliates include departmental federations of Arequipa, Cuzco, Junin and Puno; federations of food industry, shoe and leather, civil construction, bank

formation of the American Popular Revolutionary Alliance (APRA) populist movement by Victor Raul Haya de la Torre in 1924, and the creation of a radical General Confederation of Workers of Peru (CGTP) under the inspiration of the marxist Jose Carlos Mariategui in 1929. Delegates representing 50,000 workers attended the first CGTP congress in 1930. But the dictatorship of Colonel Sanchez Cerro banned all trade union activity in 1930 and the world economic depression hit Peruvian workers hard. For example, the Cerro de Pasco mining company reduced its workforce from 13,000 to 5,000. The miners of the central highlands were especially militant, but their organisations were crushed by government repression. Meanwhile, in the northern oil fields, hundreds of workers were killed in strikes and demonstrations in protest at the lowering of wages and the lengthening of working hours.

Restraints on the labour movement were relaxed after the world war during the government of Jose Luis Bustamente (1944-48). APRA was allowed to take part in political activity, and its trade union organisation, the Confederation of Workers of Peru (CTP) encouraged unionisation. This process was cut short when General Manuel Odria took power in a coup in 1948. Once again, the labour movement suffered brutal repression and many leaders were assassinated or imprisoned. APRA, which was persecuted with particular zeal by the army, was again forced to work secretly. It was not until the fall of Odria in 1956 that the labour movement was allowed to organise without prohibitive government restrictions. The late 1950s and early 1960s witnessed the emergence of stong new unions in many sectors, for instance, the mining metallurgical and fishing industries. Many of these unions also challenged the leadership of the CTP which, along with its parent APRA, had lost much of its former militancy, and a committee for the re-organisation and unification of the CTP was set up.

Agricultural workers demonstrated their militancy in a successful fight for the recognition of their unions in the sugar plantatations of the northern coast, and in the many invasions of privately owned but unused land in the highlands. The activity of the

provincial federation of the Convencion and Lares Valleys under the leadership of the

trotskyist Hugo Blanco attracted international attention before the army moved in to destroy the peasant organisation and imprison its leaders.

In 1963, the military, which had taken power in 1962 to forestall APRA winning the election, handed over to the civilian government of President Belaùnde Terry, which allowed the increasingly conservative CTP to operate, but clamped down on the more militant unions. As the economy ran into severe difficulties, the labour movement acted to protect living standards of workers, and the government moved to the right. Rather than work for the reorganisation of the CTP, the most important unions set up a new General Confederation of Workers of Peru (CGTP) in 1968 under the political leadership of the CP. Later that same year the military once again staged a coup, but this time

it was led by a group of radical nationalist officers, headed by General Juan Velasco Alvarado. Velasco himself wrote that the aim of the 1968 revolution was to create 'a social democracy of full participation' in which 'the means of production are predominantly social property' and where decisions are taken by ordinary men and women rather than political and economic oligarchies. The government nationalised the powerful United States multinational corporation, the International Petroleum Company, and introduced a series of agrarian, industrial and educational reforms. In 1970, it introduced a law giving workers greater protection from employers and greater job stability.

However, attempts to undermine the independence of the trade unions and a fall in real wages in the mid 1970s aroused the hostility of the labour movement. Many new unions were formed in this period, and the CGTP became the most powerful confederation. In 1972, the government set up its own Workers' Confederation of the Peruvian Revolution (CTRP), and Christian Democrats formed the National Confederation of Workers (CNT) in 1971. The CTRP continued to receive government support although some of its affiliates later played a role in anti-government strikes. In the first half of the 1970s, these confederations supported the government, a stance attacked by those unions which challenged the programme of the military. These dissident unions, including teachers, miners and metalworkers, formed the Committee for Class Trade Union Co-ordination and Unification (CCUSC) in 1974.

The replacement of Velasco Alvarado by the conservative General Morales Bermudez in 1975 signalled a turn to the right in which relations between the government and the labour movement sharply deteriorated. In response to falling living standards and government repression, a wave of strikes swept the country. Violence was used to crush a major strike by the strong fishermens' union in 1976, and in July of that year the government declared a state of emergency. In November the government suspended the job security law introduced in 1970. These measures set the scene for the biggest general strike in the history of the country. Although the reactionary CTP opposed the action and sectarianism prevented the participation of some important unions, the strike was an impressive display of strength by the labour movement. The strikers demanded an increase in wages in line with the increase in the cost of living, the freezing of prices of basic foodstuffs, the honouring of collective agreements, the reintroduction of job security, the reinstatement of all dismissed workers, freedom of those arrested and repatriation for those exiled, full respect for democratic rights, the solution of the fishermens' problems, the cancellation of peasant debts, and respect for the independence of the university. Several workers were killed in clashes with troops. Two days after the strike, the government issued a decree allowing private and state companies to dismiss union leaders and workers involved in the strike. The Peruvian bishops issued a statement in which they declared that the government's recent economic measures were 'disastrous for the people and only benefit a small minority. The people's lack of freedom leads them to desperation and they rebel against these injustices.' They went on to call for an 'end to repression, the release of prisoners, an end to the increasing cost of living, just prices and salaries for the peasants and workers, freedom of expression, respect for popular organisations, the re-establishment of constitutional guarantees, etc'.

The lack of unity of the labour movement and the ambiguous attitude of the CGTP weakened the hand of the workers, but the government lifted the state of emergency and, later in the year, announced the calling of a constituent assembly to prepare the ground for a return to civilian rule. Elections for the assembly reflected the mood of the working class, with left wing parties scoring unprecedented victories. Unrest continued in 1978 with a steelworkers' strike, a CGTP-led general strike, a national teachers' strike, and in September, a national miners' strike. The government declared the latter strike illegal and gave the miners three days to return to work or lose their jobs. Ten thousand miners marched to Lima to demand the release of over 200 union leaders arrested in the previous 18 months. Severe repression and the placing of five mining areas under military rule finally broke the strike despite solidarity from other unions, including bank workers and civil servants.

Despite the repression and harassment, the labour movement has continued to defend itself. The four month long teachers' strike of 1979 had wide support among the population. According to figures published by the Lima labour monthly *Jornal*, the real wages of teachers fell by 43.5% between the end of 1975 and summer 1979. However, an upturn in the economy, the granting of pay rises and the imminence of a return to civilian rule had reduced the level of social and labour unrest by the beginning of 1980.

PUERTO RICO

POPULATION	3.4 million
ECON. ACTIVE	1.0 million
UNIONISED	14% (estimate 1975)
UNEMPLOYED	25% (official 1977) 50% (NACLA 1976)
LIFE EXPECTANCY	

FEDERATIONS

FLTPR — Federacion Libre de los Trabajadores de Puerto Rico. Affil. ORIT. 105,000. Calle Fortaleza 56, Apartado 270, San Juan.

FTPR — Federacion del Trabajo de Puerto Rico (1974). Affil. AFL-CIO. 80,000. Calle Tanca 252, Avenida Ponce de Leon 804, San Juan 8.

FUTP — Frente Unido de Trabajadores Puertorriquenos. Affil. CLAT. Avenida de Diego 403, Puerto Nuevo 00917, San Juan.

UGT — Union General de Trabajadores (1948). Affil. CPUSTAL. Calle Cerra 611, Parada 15, San Turce.

The Puerto Rican trade union movement dates from the final years of the nineteenth century when the Regional Workers Federation (1898) and the Free Federation of Labour (FLT, 1899) were established. The persecution and assassination of union militants led the unions to seek the protection of the US Association of Federated Labour (AFL). The US captured Puerto Rico from Spain in the war of 1898 and US unions were henceforth to play an important role in the history of the island's labour movement, although this was often far from beneficial. They did, however, give useful support in

"Here are the facts you should know about Puerto Rico's higher productivity, lower wages and tax-free profits"

Teodoro Moscoso, Administrator of the Economic Development Administration of the Commonwealth of Puerto Rico, describes some of the major reasons behind Puerto Rico's record of consistently higher profits for manufacturers.

Read what he has to say about what this most profitable of U.S. plant sites can mean to your bottom line, then send in the coupon below for more information.

❝There is no mystery about the steady influx of U.S. manufacturers to Puerto Rico over the last 25 years. *Operation Bootstrap*, our economic self-help program, has always operated on the principle that business will go where the profits are.

Let me tell you about three major factors that continue to attract billions of dollars in manufacturing investment to Puerto Rico—total tax exemption higher worker productivity and lower labor costs.

1. Total Tax Exemption

One result of the Commonwealth of Puerto Rico's unique compact of permanent union with the United States is that U.S. Federal taxes on corporate income *do not apply* in Puerto Rico. This makes Puerto Rico the only location under the U.S. flag where corporate profits are completely free of U.S. Federal income taxes.

In addition, the Commonwealth has passed laws of its own which give your plant in Puerto Rico 100% exemption from corporate income taxes, real or personal property taxes and municipal license fees.

This exemption from Puerto Rican taxes is extended over periods of from 10 to 30 years, depending on the location of your plant on the island.

How about repatriation of profits to the U.S. mainland? If you set up your Puerto Rican operation under Section 931 of the Internal Revenue Code, you may repatriate all of your profits completely free of U.S. or Commonwealth taxes.

With unemployment in Puerto Rico now exceeding 20%, we need the jobs you can provide. To get those jobs, we have made certain that in Puerto Rico the profit you make is the profit you keep —all of it.

2. Higher Worker Productivity

Manufacturers, both U.S. and foreign, have repeatedly expressed their admiration for the skill and dedication of their workers in Puerto Rico. These qualities have meant higher manufacturing output and increased profits.

The level of worker productivity in Puerto Rico is among the highest in the

Teodoro Moscoso is Administrator of Puerto Rico's Economic Development Administration. Businessman, diplomat and government planner, he was the "father" of this U.S. island's remarkable self-help program, "Operation Bootstrap," in the mid-40's.

He served as U.S. Ambassador to Venezuela under President John F. Kennedy, was the first Coordinator of the Alliance for Progress, Chairman of the Executive Committee of the Banco de Ponce, and until 1973 he was Chairman of the Board of the Commonwealth Oil Refining Company.

world. The latest U.S. Census of Manufacturers found that a worker in Puerto Rico returns an average $4.03 in

Worker Productivity per Wage Dollar*	
(Puerto Rico vs. Major Industrial States)	
Illinois	$3.37
Michigan	$2.89
Ohio	$3.12
New York	$3.72
Pennsylvania	$2.98
New Jersey	$3.77
Massachusetts	$3.50
Louisiana	$3.99
North Carolina	$3.21
California	$3.70
U.S. National Average	$3.36
PUERTO RICO	**$4.03**

value for every dollar of wages earned.

This is well above the U.S. average of $3.36 and puts Puerto Rico among the top U.S. plant sites in labor productivity —and as the accompanying chart shows, ahead of most leading industrial states.

3. Lower Labor Costs

Although the Fair Labor Standards Act covers Puerto Rico, industrial wages on the island are much closer to the statutory minimum than any other plant site in the United States.

With a plant on the U.S. mainland, you have to contend with an average hourly wage of $5.02. In Puerto Rico, the average is $2.69—and that includes sick

leave, vacation, and paid holidays.

Why not join manufacturers in your

Comparison of Average Hourly Earnings Between Puerto Rico and U.S. Mainland*			
INDUSTRY GROUP	P. Rico Aver. Hourly Wage	U.S. Aver. Hourly Wage	Labor Cost Saved
Tobacco	$2.21	$4.82	$2.61
Textile products	2.24	3.56	1.32
Apparel	2.18	3.86	1.51
Furniture & fixtures	2.35	3.33	1.15
Printing & publishing	3.34	5.54	2.20
Chemical products	3.61	5.65	2.04
Rubber & plastic products	2.59	4.50	1.91
Leather products	2.05	3.37	1.32
Wood products	2.19	4.46	2.27
Stone, clay & glass products	3.04	5.04	2.00
Metal products	3.14	5.30	2.16
Non-electrical machinery	3.32	5.60	2.28
Electrical machinery	2.92	4.77	1.85
Transportation equipment	3.07	6.35	3.28
Scientific instruments	2.94	4.75	1.81
Miscellaneous	2.73	3.97	1.24

industry who are producing more for the dollar with a plant in Puerto Rico? ❞

Locate your industry on the profit chart and see how much your current profit margin could increase with a plant in Puerto Rico. Then send in the coupon below for our new booklet, "Fast Facts About Profits & Puerto Rico," plus a detailed fact sheet on our Industrial Incentive Act.

Mr. Teodoro Moscoso
Commonwealth of Puerto Rico
Economic Development Administration
Dept. TH-16
1290 Ave. of the Americas, N.Y., N.Y. 10019
I want to know more about Puerto Rico's total tax exemption, higher worker productivity and

these first years. In the first decade of the century labour organisations conducted a major drive to unionise sugar plantation workers but it was difficult to establish permanent organisations since the abundance of unemployed labour gave the workers a poor bargaining position. The most militant workers in this period were not on the sugar plantations but employed in the tobacco industry, 53% being women. In 1915 the Socialist Party was formed as the political wing of the FLT.

Between 1928 and 1939 income from agricultural exports dropped by 32%, unemployment soared and living standards fell dramatically. However, the plantation owners continued to make huge profits as millions of dollars' worth of sugar was exported. Outraged workers struck in 1934 in protest at this situation and in rejection of the new collective agreements signed by the FLT bureaucracy. The General Confederation of Workers (CGT) was set up in March 1940 with 112 delegates representing 42 unions. Initially a radical organisation set up by those opposed to the FLT's conciliatory policies, the CGT led many strikes especially on the plantations. However, it subsequently lost its militancy and moved closer to the government. These years witnessed the rise of the Popular Democratic Party (PPD), which came to power in 1940 with the support of the workers. Its slogan was 'land, bread and freedom'. But once in power it concentrated on attracting massive foreign investment while holding down living standards and co-opting important figures in the CGT, which split in 1945.

In 1946 the Taft Hartley Law was passed in the US Congress. This law, which also applied to Puerto Rico, outlawed secondary picketing, solidarity strikes and the closed shop, and introduced measures against unions indulging in 'unfair labour practices'. All disputes came under the jurisdiction of the US National Labour Relations Board where all hearings and statements were in English. There is widespread resentment in Puerto Rico that measures such as this are applied to the island's workers while, at the same time, they do not receive the benefits of US minimum wage legislation.

After the Second World War the Puerto Rican labour movement became increasingly dominated by US unions, in particular the International Brotherhood of Teamsters, the Seafarers International Union and the International Ladies Garments Workers Union. In 1949 the CGT affiliated to the US Congress of Industrial Organisations (CIO). In recent years some independent national unions have emerged although existing legislation and victimisation have undermined their effectiveness. The United Labour Movement (MOU), created after the Nixon wage freeze of 1971, gained the support of 42 unions and 40,000 workers but subsequently disintegrated. Its successor, the Union Committee Against Repression (CSCR), was established in 1977 after the assassination of teamster shop steward Juan Rafael Caballero who was last seen alive in a police station. The CSCR brought together 26 unions and warned the government that 'any action against a labour leader, or against a union, will constitute an act of aggression against the entire workers' movement'.

A major focus of militancy in the 1970s has been the public sector. In 1973 there were strikes by sanitation, electricity, water workers and fire fighters, necessitating the first mobilisation of the National Guard since the 1950s independence risings. In 1974 teachers, bus and truck drivers, dockers and postal workers all staged major strikes. A Personnel Law of 1975 made a government agency responsible for bargaining on behalf of public sector workers, who form about a third of the total workforce. In addition, the law guaranteed jobs only for those workers who satisfy the criteria of 'productivity, efficiency, order and discipline'. The following year Romero Barcelo won the election for Governor after promises to raise minimum wages and reform the labour law to permit freedom to unionise in the public sector. Once in office, Barcelo reneged on these pledges, fearing the spread of militant independent trade unionism in this vital area.

At the end of 1978 the government introduced a bill providing for corporate bargaining units, elaborate bureaucratic procedures for declaring strikes with the risk of substantial fines for unions, the establishment of a public sector relations board with the power to stop strikes 'affecting health or public safety or the continuation of essential public services', the prohibition of industrial action in election years, the elimination of many aspects of working conditions from negotiations, and forbidding the closed shop.

Strikes by power and public transport workers in 1978 demonstrated the militancy of public sector groups and further clashes are likely. However, the immediate likelihood of major US unions actively supporting their Puerto Rican members remains small for, although recruitment has been extensive, it has been undertaken largely in order to boost membership dues. The US steelworkers' union, for example, has Puerto Rican chapters of hospital workers, shop employees and journalists. Lack of independence thus remains a major obstacle for the Puerto Rican labour movement.

TRINIDAD AND TOBAGO

POPULATION	1.1 million
ECON. ACTIVE	400,000
UNIONISED	
UNEMPLOYED	12.2% (1978)
LIFE EXPECTANCY	67.5 years

MAJOR UNIONS

ATSEFTWU — All Trinidad Sugar Estates and Factory Workers Trade Union.

ICFTU — Island Wide Cane Farmers Trade Union.

OWTU — Oil Workers Trade Union.

SISA — Sugar Industry Staff Association.

TIWU — Transport and Industrial Workers Union.

Riots on the waterfront of the capital, Port of Spain, in 1919 gave notice of the birth of the labour movement in Trinidad. The associated strike was organised by the Working Men's Reform Club and the Trinidad Working Men's Association. However, the British colonial administration was able to keep attempts at organisation of the workers in close check and it was not until the 1930s that further advances of substance were made. During the unrest of the inter-war years the Negro Welfare Association took the leadership of the northern oil workers and the Uriah Butler Movement was instrumental in organising the sugar plantation workers. But the British were ready to use force to halt these moves and the hunger marches of 1934 and riots of 1937 were brutally repressed.

When Elma Francois, a prominent labour leader, was put on trial for 'agitation' and asked by the prosecutor why she persisted in making speeches which were 'causing disaffection among his Majesty's subjects', she replied, 'I don't know that my speeches cause disaffection. I know that my speeches create a fire in the minds of the people so as to change the conditions which now exist'. Rhetoric such as this found a receptive audience and the post-war period saw the formation of the militant OWTU and sugar workers' unions. Nevertheless, independence was not to be granted until 1962 and when, in 1965, there was a major strike for better conditions this was suppressed by the government of Eric Williams with the use of troops. A state of emergency was declared and an Industrial Stabilisation Act (ISA), which was rushed through parliament, effectively banned all strikes.

The authoritarian and anti-working class nature of Williams' government drew increasing opposition and in 1968 the OWTU and the TIWU formed the Council of Progressive Trade Unions. Two years later massive worker demonstrations supported by elements within the army were put down by the regime and another state of emergency declared. An industrial relations act replaced the ISA in 1972 and in 1975 all the major unions (oil, sugar, electrical and transport) formed an alliance called the United Labour Front (ULF) to fight the 1976 elections. But racial differences and disagreements over policy led to the division of the body.

The continued rule of Williams' People's National Movement (PNM) has sustained political and labour unrest but the ULF remains split into radical and moderate factions, although even the leader of the moderates, Basdeo Panday, asserts that 'democracy is dead' in Trinidad and Tobago. The PNM economic strategy has been to rely on earnings from oil, which accounts for 91% of exports, and encourage foreign investment which, lured by low wages and generous concessions, has been flooding in. This, however, has done little to off-set severe economic difficulties which, combined with a powerful movement for independence in Tobago, have increased tension. In Christmas 1979 there were bomb attacks on the Texaco refinery and the PNM headquarters, and in March 1980 another on the minister of housing, most probably in retaliation for the government's forcible disbanding of a squatter settlement on the outskirts of Port of Spain. Under such conditions Trinidad and Tobago look set for further and increased political struggles in which the recent establishment of more radical governments in the Caribbean will provide encouragement for the labour movement.

URUGUAY

POPULATION	2.8 million (1978)
ECON. ACTIVE	1.1 million (1978)
UNIONISED	
UNEMPLOYED	10.1% (1978)
LIFE EXPECTANCY	72.0 years

CONFEDERATIONS

CNT — Convencion Nacional de Trabajo (1964). Affil. CPUSTAL. Illegal.

CGTU — Confederacion General de Trabajadores de Uruguay (1973). Government-backed body.

The history of the Uruguayan labour movement goes back to the 1880s when immigration from Europe and economic development gave a strong impetus to the growth of trade unions. The first national labour congress was held in 1896, but strikes were met with severe repression. At the turn of the century there were 28 unions in the capital, Montevideo, and 11 more in the provinces. The first national confederations emerged in the first decade of this century. The Central Union of Workers (UGT) was established in 1902 and the Regional Labour Federation of Uruguay (FORU) was established in 1905.

The governments of President Batlle (1903-07 and 1911-15) established an advanced social security system and passed a labour law recognising basic trade union freedoms, although public service workers were denied the right to strike. In 1915 Uruguay became the first country on the continent to institute the eight hour working day.

The increased rate of economic development stimulated by the world demand for wool and beef during the First World War accelerated the growth of the labour movement with the maritime workers' union emerging as one of the strongest unions. Workers continued to organise but the movement was badly split along political lines at this time. The economic problems caused by the world depression led to a coup in 1933, the only instance of a breakdown in constitutional rule that Uruguay was to suffer this century before the military coup of 1973. This was a difficult time for the labour movement. The confederations declined in influence and most unions operated in isolation.

However, with the economic recovery of the 1940s the degree of unionisation increased rapidly. The main unions were those formed by meat packers, textile workers, engineers, railwaymen, dockers, construction workers in the capital and various groups of agricultural workers. Unionisation was particularly strong in nationalised industries and the welfare state

Since the military coup in 1973 one in every fifty Uruguayans has been arrested for political reasons.

The congress which established the CNT in 1964, a major advance in the history of the Uruguayan labour movement. In 1973 the CNT was outlawed, thousands of members arrested, and eighteen members of the CNT Central Council "disappeared".

institutions — oil and electrical workers, teachers, national health employees and civil servants.

The period 1940-55 was a time of increasing prosperity for Uruguay, which was reflected in rising wage levels. Between 1948-54, the cost of living went up by 58% but the wages of workers in 31 trade unions increased by 110%. The labour movement was able to develop its organisations and gain experience in liberal political conditions relatively free of the close state control experienced by the Brazilian and Argentinian labour movements under Vargas and Peron respectively or the repression that faced workers elsewhere in Latin America.

The economic situation began to deteriorate in the mid-1950s. Since the beginning of the century, and particularly since the Second World War, the income from wool and meat exports had made Uruguay a comparatively rich country. This wealth had been used to create extensive welfare state, finance industrialisation and develop the national health and education systems. Now the international terms of trade began to worsen and the stagnation of production in the rural sector, due largely to lack of investment, became apparent. The country entered a period of severe economic crisis; the cost of living doubled between 1955 and 1959.

The unions mobilised to defend their living standards; a series of strikes indicated the growing restlessness of workers and the conservative pro-US Union Confederation of Uruguay (CSU) lost what little influence it had. Meanwhile, the Single Workers' Centre (CUT) grew in strength. By 1962, it had 50,000 members and grouped all important unions. In 1964 the National Confederation of Labour (CNT) was established, bringing together all the major unions in the country.

The inflationary spiral continued and industrial unrest increased in proportion. Inflation was 100% in 1965 and

140% in 1967. In the face of this economic crisis the CNT proposed a programme aimed at changing the structure of the economy through nationalisation of the most important sectors. However, the government of President Pacheco Areco, who came to office in 1967, imposed a wage freeze and devalued the currency. The workers' standard of living began to fall drastically, but the government took an increasingly firm stand in labour disputes and troops were used to break strikes by meatpackers, electrical and bank workers.

The official reason for the introduction of new security laws was the need to combat the Tupamaros guerillas who had taken up arms in response to the government's economic policies and the repression of the labour movement. In reality, the security measures were aimed at stifling the opposition of ordinary shop floor workers. In 1971, attention was transferred to general elections. It is generally acknowledged that the official winner, Juan Bordaberry, was involved in electoral fraud, and that Wilson Ferreira Aldunate, who had promised major reforms and a return to constitutional rule, was the real victor. Bordaberry continued with the same policies as Pacheco but now the military became more directly involved in national politics through the fight against the Tupamaros and the repression of the labour movement.

In February 1973 the generals presented Bordaberry with an ultimatum demanding the formation of a Council of National Security. The labour movement was confused and divided on how to react to the army's 16 point programme, which called for land reform, an end to corruption, and a specific refusal to be used by the government against the trade unions. The pattern of events became clearer in June 1973 when Bordaberry and the armed forces agreed to close down congress, outlaw political parties, ban public meetings and suspend the constitution. The CNT responded immediately by calling a general strike. It demanded the restoration of all constitutional guarantees and political rights, economic measures to deal with the crisis including the nationalisation of the banks, an increase in real wages and respect for trade union rights. Bordaberry decreed the dissolution of the CNT, closed down its offices and arrested union leaders.

Workers occupied the factories and came out onto the streets to protest. Factories were cleared by troops and then re-occupied by workers, sometimes four or five times. Despite their courage and tenacity, the workers could do nothing in the face of tanks and armoured cars. The demonstrations continued but the army gradually assumed control and rounded up union leaders and militants. After 15 days the CNT leadership called off the strike in the hope that some compromise might be achieved, but it was not to be. Employers took advantage of the situation to annul collective contracts, dismiss militants and collaborate with the army to round up trade union officials.

Generalised repression, torture, imprisonment, exile, unemployment and low living standards have been the lot of the vast majority of Uruguayans since 1973. The labour movement has suffered a two-fold attack. First, physical intimidation, including the most barbaric torture, is the standard weapon used by the military government against workers who seek to organise opposition to the regime. Second, blacklists and dismissal are used to root out militant elements. In addition, the government has made attempts to set up a parallel union structure through the CGTU, but this has patently failed to win the support of most workers. Meanwhile, the CNT maintains a clandestine structure and a leadership in exile. In these circumstances, resistance is often only an isolated act of defiance. For example, workers at the state electricity company have caused power cuts in protest at the dictatorship, but there has been no significant strike in the last three years.

Between 1971 and 1976 the fall in real wages was 35%, and in 1979 inflation was 80% while wage increases were only 45%. Meanwhile defence spending has increased from some 8% of the state budget in 1976 to an estimated 50% in 1979. In May 1979, after long delays, the draft text of the new labour code was revealed. The main aim of the new legislation was 'to replace the concept of class struggle and the national disunity it implies, with co-operation between capital and labour'. Candidates for union office will have to sign a 'declaration of democratic faith' and each union must provide a list of all union members. Each union will also have to provide reports on its activities at the request of the ministry of labour, and all unions will be banned from political activity. The labour code has been strongly condemned by the ILO, and within Uruguay the bank workers union distributed a document outlining their reasons for totally rejecting it.

The Uruguayan working class suffered a major defeat with the military coup of 1973. Since then the recovery of independent labour organisation has been very slight indeed. Perhaps nowhere else in Latin America has military dictatorship rooted itself so totally and the struggle to bring down the regime will be long and arduous.

VENEZUELA

POPULATION	12.9 million (1977)
ECON. ACTIVE	4.1 million (1978)
UNIONISED	45%
UNEMPLOYED	4.8% (1977)
LIFE EXPECTANCY	66.4 years

CONFEDERATIONS

CODESA — Confederation de Sindicatos Autonomos de Venezuela (1964). Affil. CLAT. Estimated membership 10,000, claims 35,000. 120 local unions including textile, petrol distribution, public health and education workers federations. Dominated by COPEI political party. Edificio Don Miguel, Esquina Cipreses, Caracas DF.

CTV — Confederacion de Trabajadores de Venezuela (1947) Affil. ORIT. Edificio CTV, Esquina Lienda Honda, Apartado 8056, Caracas DF. Estimated membership 1,100,000, claims two million. 68 regional and industrial federations with over 6,000 unions. Includes FCV (peasants) 700,000; FETRACONS (construction workers) 100,000; FETRASALUD (health workers) 45,000; FETRAMETAL (metal workers and miners) 32,000; FEDEPETROL (oil workers) only 6,000 but the strongest union in the country; Federacion Venezolana de Maestros (teachers).

A fifteen member executive council represents all the major political parties but the CTV is dominated by Accion Democratica. Affiliates comprise over 90% of organised labour. Dissolved 1949 and reconstituted 1959.

CUTV — Confederacion Unitaria de Trabajadores Venezolanos (1963) Affil. CPUSTAL. Avenida Lecuna, Edificio Trinidad-Mezanina, Caracas DF. Estimated membership 40,000, claims 100,000. Eight regional and five industrial federations (textiles, flour, sugar, printing and white collar workers) in 185 local unions. Membership concentrated amongst poorly paid sectors.

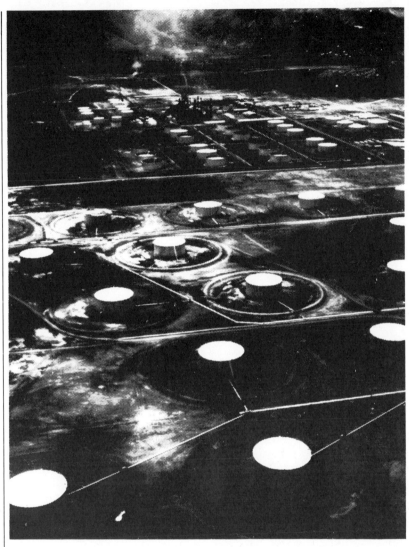

The early development of the Venezuelan labour movement was severely hampered by the long dictatorship of Juan Vicente Gomez (1908-35). Mutualist societies and trade unions were forced to maintain a semi-clandestine existence even though Venezuela was one of the founder members of the International Labour Organisation. The first attempts at organisation on a national level came in 1919 when rail, telephone and power workers were instrumental in establishing the General Labour Confederation. The most important focus of labour unrest in the 1920s was the oil industry. The oil multinationals were virtually a law unto themselves and living conditions in the company towns were appalling. Early demands were for running water and adequate sanitation but only small advances were made despite strike action. An oil workers' union established in 1931 was crushed and its leaders imprisoned a few days before strike action was to be taken. The only concessions made by Gomez came in 1928 after student demonstrations set off a general strike which threatened to overthrow the regime. However, repression continued until the death of Gomez at the end of 1935. When his successor, General Contreras, continued in the same vein, a general strike was called to demand the end of press censorship, the repeal of the act suspending constitutional guarantees, democratisation of the country, the freeing of political prisoners, and the sacking of officials who had supported the Gomez dictatorship. The government replied with repression, killing 23 people; but after 30,000 people had demonstrated in front of the National Palace and angry crowds burned down or ransacked 500 houses belonging to government supporters, the government backed down. A labour code was promulgated, with provisions for an eight hour day and the legal recognition of unions. By December 1936 113 unions had been formed. Social security measures were decreed and supporters of the dictatorship were forced out of office.

However, Contreras soon clamped down on the labour movement, imprisoned or exiled trade union leaders, and banned the holding of the second national workers' congress in 1938. It was not until General Medina Angarita came to power in 1941, that the labour movement was able to organise freely again. Labour organisation was given a strong impetus after a coup, backed by the recently formed Accion Democratica party (AD), took place in 1945. In three years, the number of unions quadrupled and at a national workers' congress in 1947 the Confederation of Workers of Venezuela (CTV)

was formed. Agricultural workers were organised for the first time and their unions were recognised by the government. This period saw substantial increases in real wages and advances in the organisation of regional and industrial labour federations. This favourable political climate was short-lived. In 1948 General Perez Jimenez, backed by the army and conservative social forces threatened by the development of the labour movement, overthrew President Romulo Gallegos.

A strike by oil workers in opposition to the coup was broken by the dictatorship, which proceeded to dismantle all trade union organisation and dissolve the CTV. All authentic trade union activity was repressed for a decade, although Perez Jimenez made attempts to set up a subservient national trade union organisation. At an international oil conference held in Caracas in 1956, a Dutch labour delegate spoke out against the repression of the labour movement in the presence of the dictator himself. The conference was immediately suspended, and Venezuela withdrew from the ILO, which had sponsored the conference.

When Perez Jimenez fell from power in 1958 following mounting civilian and military opposition, the labour movement was quick to re-organise after years of clandestine activity. A National Committee of Trade Union Unity was formed, containing representatives from all political parties. It began the task of creating strong trade union organisations, and mobilised the workers in defence of the new democratic government when it was threatened by another coup within a year of being in office. When the CTV was re-established an attempt was made to preserve labour unity by including representatives of all political parties on

the national executive. Although the social democratic Accion Democratica had the closest relationship with the unions, it was recognised that workers were also influenced by the Christian Democrat party, COPEI, and the Communist Party.

This labour unity was maintained until the regime had consolidated itself. Meanwhile, unions and federations multiplied in number, and earlier labour legislation was reactivated. During the presidencies of Romulo Betancourt (1958-64) and Raul Leoni (1964-68), both members of AD, the CTV maintained close relations with the government and, in 1963, expelled communist unions who then formed the Unitary Confederation of Workers of Venezuela (CUTV). The government was the most important source of financial support for the unions, and provided the CTV with national and regional offices.

The number of strikes increased markedly during the presidency of the Christian Democrat, Rafael Caldera (1968-73), but this was the result of the unions' political opposition to a more conservative government rather than an indication of declining living standards or attacks on the labour movement. In fact, Venezuela has had the most stable system of government and industrial relations in South America over the last 20 years. There was significant labour unrest in the iron and steel and oil industries after they were nationalised in 1975 and 1976 respectively, but the only generalised discontent occurred towards the end of 1979, under the Christian Democrat government of Luis Herrera Campins (1979-).

The reason for this stability is the economic progress enjoyed by Venezuela thanks to its huge oil reserves. Wages are the highest in Latin America, there is a high turnover of labour, and a corresponding rate of absenteeism. Since the Constitution guaranteed basic trade union rights in 1961, individual laws and decrees have introduced various fringe benefits for workers and given other limited guarantees. Social security provisions took effect in 1967 although the system does not cover the entire country. In 1976 the government created a commission to study the enrolment of the peasants into the system. A 1974 law gave further protection against unfair dismissals, and a 1975 law instituted profit sharing.

However, the executive has the power to recognise unions and to dissolve them. The right to strike is severely restricted in law. In any dispute, arbitration procedures are mandatory. Of the 282 strikes which took place in 1975-76 only four were declared to be legal. This has not, of course, stopped workers striking or winning wage increases through industrial action, but in less favourable political and economic con-

ditions the full force of the law could be used against any workers in dispute with their employers. Employees in the public sector are at a further disadvantage, for they do not have the legal right to strike. If they cannot agree on a collective contract within 90 days, the matter is referred to a government committee weighted against workers. There is no appeal against the committee's decision. Another major restraint on the labour movement

is the bureaucratic nature of the CTV, and its close relationship with Accion Democratica. Its leaders are mostly professionals with generous wages rather than worker representatives drawn from the shop floor. Workers taking industrial action are likely to find themselves faced with opposition from the CTV as well as the government and employees.

The control of the CTV by Accion Democratica, now in opposition, and a sharp increase in the rate of inflation has combined to bring the labour movement on to the streets to protest at the government's economic policies. Over 1,000 collective wage contracts were due for renewal in 1979, and workers were adamant that settlements should reflect the rise in the inflation rate.

The violent dispersal of a workers' demonstration in Caracas, and the death of a worker in clashes with the police in Valencia during a one day strike in October 1979 brought the threat of a general strike. The government's agreement to reinstate 700 textile workers sacked during the disturbances and a victory for the CTV wage proposals defused the tensions. A coalition of left-wing parties in the national congress outvoted the government and passed the CTV's wages bill, thus making the public and private sector companies legally obliged to make full allowance for the rate of inflation when drawing up new collective contracts.

Further labour unrest is likely under this government, and there has even been speculation that a military coup is in the offing. At the moment, however, this seems unlikely and the principal objective of the labour movement is to defend its economic and political position within the broad framework of political liberalism.

Venezuelan dockers impose boycott on Chilean cargoes.

USEFUL ADDRESSES

AMNESTY INTERNATIONAL – BRITISH SECTION, Tower House, 8-14 Southampton Street, London WC2E 7HF. Tel: (01) 836 5621

AMNESTY INTERNATIONAL SECRETARIAT, 10 Southampton Street, London WC2E 7HF. Tel: (01) 836 7788

ANTI-SLAVERY SOCIETY FOR THE PROTECTION OF HUMAN RIGHTS, 60 Weymouth Street, London W1N 4DX. Tel: (01) 935 Tel: (01) 935 6498

COMMITTEE FOR THE DEFENCE OF BOLIVIAN DEMOCRACY, c/o CALA, 1 Cambridge Terrace, London NW1 4JL.

BRITISH ARGENTINA CAMPAIGN, c/o 1 Cambridge Terrace, London NW1 4JL.

CARIBBEAN LABOUR SOLIDARITY, 138 Southgate Road, London N1.

CENTRAL AMERICA HUMAN RIGHTS COMMITTEE, c/o 59a Church Street, Old Isleworth, Middlesex TW7 6BE.

CHILE COMMITTEE FOR HUMAN RIGHTS (CCHR), 1 Cambridge Terrace, London NW1 4JL. Tel: (01) 935 5953

CHILE SOLIDARITY CAMPAIGN (CSC), 129 Seven Sisters Road, London N7 7QG. Tel: (01) 272 4299

COMMITTEE FOR HUMAN RIGHTS IN ARGENTINA (CHRA), 1 Cambridge Terrace, London NW1 4JL. Tel: (01) 486 4980

COMMITTEE FOR HUMAN RIGHTS IN URUGUAY (CHRI-U), 1 Cambridge Terrace, London NW1 4JL.

COMMITTEE FOR PUERTO RICAN INDEPENDENCE, BM-CPRI, London WC1V 6XX.

CONTEMPORARY ARCHIVE ON LATIN AMERICA (CALA), 1 Cambridge Terrace, London NW1 4JL. Tel: (01) 487 5277

JOINT WORKING GROUP FOR REFUGEES FROM LATIN AMERICA, 266 Pentonville Road, London N1. Tel: (01) 278 3329

LATIN AMERICA BUREAU (LAB), PO Box 134, London NW1 4JY. Tel: (01) 486 1730

LATIN AMERICAN SOLIDARITY FRONT, 107 Harehill Avenue, Leeds 8. Tel: (0532) 629631

LATIN AMERICAN WOMEN'S GROUP, c/o Carila, 29 Islington Park Street, London N1.

LIBERATION, 313-315 Caledonian Road, London N1. Tel: (01) 607 0465.

LIBERATION BRAZIL COMMITTEE, 10 Rodrick Road, London NW3 2NL.

NICARAGUA SOLIDARITY CAMPAIGN, c/o 20-21 Compton Terrace, London N1 2UN. Tel: (01) 226 6747

PARAGUAY COMMITTEE FOR HUMAN RIGHTS, 15 Burford Gardens, London N13 4LR.

PARLIAMENTARY HUMAN RIGHTS GROUP, House of Commons, London SW1AA 0AA. Tel: (01) 219 5705

SOLIDARITY COMMITTEE WITH POLITICAL PRISONERS IN MEXICO, c/o Centro Iberico, 421 Harrow Road, London W9.